New Orleans Style

Past & Present

New Orleans Style
Past & Present

Susan Sully

Photographs by Paula Illingworth
and Susan Sully

Foreword by Patricia H. Gay,
PRESERVATION RESOURCE CENTER OF NEW ORLEANS

RIZZOLI
NEW YORK

ENDPAPERS:

Reception hall, Durant
DaPonte House, St. Charles
Avenue, designed by New
Orleans architect Thomas
O. Sully, c. 1890s. Used
with permission from
Southeastern Architectural
Archive, Special Collections,
Tulane University Library.

PAGES 2–3:
New Orleans architect
Samuel Wilson designed
this neo-Palladian tea
house in 1959 for the
Strachan family's Garden
District house.

PAGE 4: Mardi Gras
expert Henri Schindler
decorated his parlor
mantel as an altar to the
Greek god Proteus and an
homage to the eponymous
Carnival krewe.

PAGE 8: A cut glass
decanter, c. 1810, is part of
the collection of Sun Oak
Gardens, House Museum,
and Guest House in
Faubourg Marigny.

This book is dedicated with love to my husband, Thomas Alfred Sully III, who shares my passion for the architecture and ethos of New Orleans and with gratitude to the many preservationists who have protected New Orleans from the ravages of time and thoughtless change.

—⁘—

FIRST PUBLISHED IN THE UNITED STATES OF AMERICA IN 2004
by Rizzoli International Publications, Inc.
300 Park Avenue South, New York, NY 10010
www.rizzoliusa.com

Rizzoli Editor: Ellen R. Cohen

ISBN: 0–8478–2662–7
Library of Congress Control Number: 2004092391

Copyright © 2004 Rizzoli International Publications, Inc.
Text copyright © 2004 Susan Sully
Photography (except where noted) © 2004 Paula Illingworth
Photography on pages 8, 16, 17, 48–49, 54, 58, 59, 98, 130, 133, 140–41, 144, 157, 158, 183, 192, 197, 200, 203, 205 © 2004 Susan Sully
Foreword copyright © 2004 Patricia H. Gay
Designed by Element group

Printed in China

IT IS NOT AN EASY THING TO DESCRIBE ONE'S first impression of New Orleans; for while it actually resembles no other city upon the face of the earth, yet it recalls vague memories of a hundred cities. It owns suggestions of towns in Italy, and in Spain, of cities in England and in Germany, of seaports in the Mediterranean, and of seaports in the tropics. . . . I fancy that the power of fascination which New Orleans exercises upon foreigners is due no less to this peculiar characteristic than to the tropical beauty of the city itself. Whencesoever the traveler may have come, he may find in the Crescent City some memory of his home—some recollection of his Fatherland—some remembrance of something he loves. . . .

— LAFCADIO HEARN, 1887

Contents ──⊛──

Preserving New Orleans ———∿———

YEARS AGO, NATIONALLY SYNDICATED COLUMNIST NEIL PEARCE VISITED NEW ORLEANS. He made a remark that took us aback, looking as we were for a comment about how unique our beloved city is. "All cities are alike," he said. Surely not! Provoked into thought, we realized that most cities do indeed share many issues and require similar dynamics to protect their identities. But that brought us back to a conviction of our own and other cities' uniqueness.

New Orleans has done well in preserving what makes it special, beginning in 1936 with the establishment of the Vieux Carré Commission. This commission formed the cornerstone of a remarkable preservation movement that has developed, neighborhood by neighborhood, during the last six decades. As a result, most of historic New Orleans' charming neighborhoods remain fairly intact, despite challenge and change.

As America's fifth largest city throughout most of the nineteenth century, New Orleans was blessed with thousands of unique dwellings, from Creole cottages and shotgun houses to majestic mansions. Collectively, these buildings and their neighborhoods define the ethnically, sociologically, and stylistically complex culture that is New Orleans' legacy. Individually, they tell the stories of particular groups of people, the times they lived, their personal hopes, and their communal aspirations.

Since World War II, New Orleans, like other American cities, has been under attack. In the name of progress, neighborhoods have been brutally bulldozed, landmarks have been leveled, urban populations have declined, and interstate highways have slashed through the essence of our civilization. Recognizing the federal government's role in this devastation, Congress passed the National Preservation Act in 1964 to stem the tide of destructive projects utilizing federal funds and programs. Since then, public and private preservation programs have proliferated to save what remains of the historic built environment that defines our country.

Much harm had been done, particularly in inner-city residential neighborhoods like New Orleans' Faubourg Tremé, where a magnificent park of live oak trees was flattened to make way for an overhead expressway. The trend had to be reversed if the New Orleans loved by so many was to survive. Fortunately, such threats lent momentum to the preservation ethic. The Friends of the Cabildo was formed in 1956 to focus on the city's Spanish colonial landmarks, and the Louisiana Landmarks Society came into being the following year to protect historic sites statewide. The 1970s saw the establishment of the New Orleans Historic

District Landmarks Commission, which encouraged the creation of historic districts throughout metropolitan New Orleans.

In 1974, the Preservation Resource Center of New Orleans (PRC) was created to build the city's awareness of its valuable neighborhoods and to support the repopulation and preservation of these vulnerable areas. In the past three decades miracles have happened. A host of neighborhoods has awakened to their own identities. Some have acquired names for the first time, many reviving the lovely French word for neighborhood, *faubourg*. Thousands of threatened properties have been restored and many historic neighborhoods are thriving, with others on their way.

Cities can indeed learn from each other, and the National Trust for Historic Preservation provides a network for preservation organizations to share their ideas. A major PRC strategy is to generate awareness of the aesthetic and economic importance of historic architecture and neighborhoods. To this end, one of our earliest projects was the purchase and restoration of a nineteenth-century townhouse on Julia Street as a mixed-use space including PRC's offices.

Today, the once blighted Julia Street area is thriving with rehabilitated structures housing residences, restaurants (including Emeril Lagasse's first), galleries, hotels, offices, and other activities. PRC has since outgrown its Julia Street quarters and renovated another building in the nearby Historic Warehouse District. Like the Julia Street project, this location was chosen to anchor an endangered part of New Orleans' downtown business district, now becoming known as The American Sector.

Another PRC goal is to purchase, restore, and sell properties in declining areas in order to eliminate blight, increase homeownership, and promote neighborhood associations. Programs including "Shotgun House Month" and "The Great Neighborhood Sellabration" help attract prospective homeowners. Through Rebuilding Together, volunteer teams paint and repair homes of low-income elderly and disabled homeowners. PRC also calls attention to the rich cultural heritage of the city, restoring the former homes of jazz legends, including Kid Ory and Henry "Red" Allen, and placing historic markers on the homes of the city's jazz greats.

On the occasion of PRC's thirtieth anniversary, I hope readers around the world may learn from New Orleans, as we have learned from others. New Orleans style is alive and well, thanks to a host of organizations, city agencies, and individuals. I encourage you to join the effort to preserve what makes New Orleans, and America's other great cities, unique for future generations.

PATRICIA H. GAY, *Executive Director, Preservation Resource Center of New Orleans*

ABOVE: An intact block of late nineteenth-century shotgun houses in Faubourg Tremé reveals the work of dedicated preservationists.

New Orleans: Past and Present ———◦——

EVERY HOUSE TELLS A STORY. IN NEW ORLEANS, EACH HOUSE TELLS AT LEAST THREE: the personal history of the people who built and inhabited it; the anthropological account of its residents' social and ethnic backgrounds; and the urban evolution of the neighborhood where it stands. A veritable babel of history emanates from the façades that line the city's streets, joined by the whispered cadences of courtyards and back-buildings concealed behind them or the direct cajoling of bright gardens surrounding them. While this kind of architectural polyphony is not limited to New Orleans, there is no other city in America where it is so rich and varied.

One reason for the complexity of New Orleans' domestic environment is the immensely diverse ethnicity of its populace, who imported French, Spanish, Canadian, African, Caribbean, British, Irish, German, and Italian influences, as well as those of America's southern, midwestern, and northeastern regions. Throughout much of the nineteenth century, New Orleans was the largest port of embarkation in America after New York. Settlers came in cycles that paralleled the booms and busts of the mercurial city, leaving behind an architectural residue of houses, both modest and extravagant, that reflect a full range of styles from the eighteenth through the twenty-first century. The shape of the city, a long crescent squeezed between a lake and a river bend, necessitated that these residents establish an arc of contiguous yet discrete neighborhoods, each with distinctly different architectural and sociological characters.

While the decorated edifices of the uptown neighborhoods gesticulate boldly to one another across St. Charles Avenue, the plainer Creole structures downriver often shutter their street-side windows, turning inward upon secluded courtyards. And yet, these French Quarter houses reach across the sidewalks with iron balconies and galleries that bridge family life with city life, while the iron fences walling uptown residences establish definite boundaries between the two. This is just one of myriad examples of the complexity of New Orleans architecture and urban design—a densely woven textile embellished with bands of varied pattern in which the evolving history of the city is enmeshed.

The nexus of this tapestry is the Vieux Carré, the grid of intersecting streets laid out by French surveyor Adrien de Pauger in 1721. These streets conform to a plan designed by Pierre le Blond de la Tour for the city founded in 1718 by Jean-Baptiste Le Moyne in a bend in the Mississippi River. Sited by an overland portage and bayou connecting the river to Lake Pontchartrain, which in turn flows into the Gulf of Mexico, this spot represented a strategic link between France's Canadian and Caribbean colonies. Named for the Duke of Orleans, who was the Regent of France prior to the reign of Louis XV, the swampy settlement was touted as a New World paradise. Military personnel were dispatched to protect it from Indian, English, and Spanish threats, and land grants were handed out to noble families. These colonists were joined by slaves, indentured servants, and working class hopefuls in what began as little more than a military encampment with primitive one-story houses constructed of wood directly upon the soggy soil.

Despite many challenges, New Orleans thrived, attracting new settlers who established mercantile businesses, sugar plantations, and the necessary building trades until the population reached nearly 5,000[1] by the close of the French Colonial era in 1763. During that time, New Orleans developed its enduring reputation for exuberant social life and pleasurable pursuits, thanks in large part to the French nobility, who imported their love of fancy dress balls and opera, as well as the pomp and rituals of Catholic faith. The subtropical torpor of the region inspired a lazy sensuality; the intimate scale of the city fostered a vibrant street life; and the constant risk of decimation through fire, fever, flood, hurricanes, or warfare fed a *carpe diem* approach to life—all factors that continue to find expression in New Orleans' collective sensibility.

The French, particularly the Creoles (a term referring to people of French or Spanish antecedents born in the Indies or other New World colonies), also established architectural traditions that contributed lasting legacies to the city's built environment within, and beyond, the Vieux Carré, or French Quarter, as the area of the original city came to be known. Due to the devastation of two eighteenth-century fires, the only known remaining structures from the French Colonial period are a scattering of plantations in outlying areas and, within city bounds, the Ursuline Convent. These structures reveal certain preferences that later flourished in the Creole cottages and townhouses of the French Quarter and nearby faubourgs, as the city's neighborhoods are called.

The most enduring of these are *galleries*, as the French settlers called porches; *cabinets* (pronounced cabinā in the French manner), the name given to extensions housing storage, service rooms, additional sleeping quarters, or staircases, which stood like parentheses embracing rear galleries; and a hall-less arrangement of interconnecting rooms. While historians have variously attributed this interior plan to continental France, French–Canada, and French–Caribbean colonies, there is general agreement that the use of galleries, whether wrapping around houses on several sides or paralleling a single façade, was imported from the Caribbean.

OPPOSITE: The spires of St. Louis Cathedral, designed by J. N. B. de Pouilly and completed in 1851, tower above the broad paths of Jackson Square, in the heart of the French Quarter.

[1]Malcolm Heard, *French Quarter Manual: An Architectural Guide to New Orleans' Vieux Carré* (New Orleans: Tulane School of Architecture, 1997), p. 3.

14

"The appendage of galleries gave open-air living and sleeping space to houses while shading their openings from the sun and allowing them to remain open during rains," explains architectural historian Malcolm Heard in his *French Quarter Manual: An Architectural Guide to New Orleans' Vieux Carré.*[2]

During the French Colonial days, the city's streetscape was a staccato arrangement of freestanding houses, some low to the ground, others built upon high foundations that raised them above the flood-prone streets. The blocks, nicknamed *îles,* or islands, were surrounded by drainage ditches. Cypress planks, called *banquettes,* crossed these and provided walkways. The more familiar glissando arrangement of contiguous buildings and stuccoed walls, with the overhead flourishes of wrought-iron balconies, dates from the Spanish Colonial period, which took place from 1763 to 1802, after Louis XV ceded France's holdings along the Mississippi River to his Spanish Bourbon cousin, King Carlos III.

Historians agree that the cultural and architectural impact of the Spanish Colonial period was small, compared to the dominant French culture. Architectural historian Roulhac Toledano offers one reason why this forty-year period left so little imprint in her book, *The National Trust Guide to New Orleans.* "Most Spaniards who came to New Orleans arrived in some official capacity: as soldiers, customs officials, notaries, or government personnel, and most of those arrived without wives. This circumstance positioned the French to preserve their culture in Louisiana, beginning in the nursery after New Orleans French colonial women married Spanish men. . . . French culture continued in New Orleans, far more relaxed and sparkling, and far less religious than the usual Spanish colonial life across the New World."[3]

However, the Spanish Cabildo, as the colonial governing body was called, did succeed in making a lasting contribution to the architecture and urban structure of New Orleans following the fires of 1788 and 1794. These devastating conflagrations fed upon the wood walls and shingle roofs that were prevalent in early New Orleans architecture, spurring the Cabildo to pass new building regulations. These included requirements that houses taller than one story be built of brick or brick-between-posts, a method combining soft local brick with reinforcing cypress timbers. The new mandates dictated that exterior walls of the latter material be

BELOW: Architect Frank Masson re-created chair railings and baseboards using samples of extant moldings in the Creole cottage he and his wife Ann restored. A silver-glazed ceramic penholder, kerosene lamp, and cat skull—all nineteenth-century accoutrements—sit atop a simple Louisiana table.

[2]Ibid, p. 19.

[3]Roulhac Toledano, *The National Trust Guide to New Orleans: The Definitive Guide to Architectural and Cultural Treasures* (New York: John Wiley & Sons, 1996), p. 7.

covered with plaster and that the more steeply pitched hipped roofs favored by French colonials be replaced with relatively flat roofs covered with tile or brick.

According to Heard, "[c]onventional wisdom has it that the Spanish introduced the courtyard to New Orleans" as well.[4] "The Spanish Colonial courtyard is reached," Heard writes, ". . . by entering a carriageway cut through the volume of the building. At the end of the carriageway is another covered space, a loggia, which is open to the courtyard through breaks, often arches, in a thick stuccoed brick wall. The loggia contains the stairway to the upper residential part of the house, leaving the front rooms at street level for commercial use or the exercise of a trade." The houses of the Spanish Colonial period also featured wrought-iron balconies and tall windows fitted with louvered shutters that allowed greater control of air and light than the solid board-and-batten shutters favored by the French.

The political turmoil across the Atlantic in 1802, as Napoleon took over leadership of France, defeated Spain, and launched war against England, affected two more rapid changes in Louisiana's fortunes. The New World territory briefly regained French colonial status before being sold to the United States in 1803 through President Thomas Jefferson's Louisiana Purchase. And yet, New Orleans remained quite Gallic in culture, as Toledano explains: "New Orleans . . . reinstated French culture. As much of the Spanish population as could afford it left for Cuba. The language reverted to French both in official documents and in society."[5]

As the decades of the new century passed, these French and Spanish architectural legacies blended with the continued influence of citizens from the Caribbean (particularly those from the embattled colony of St. Domingue) to form Creole architecture—a combination of building forms and decorative traditions unique to New Orleans. Creole cottages, typically one-and-a-half story buildings with louvered shutters covering their ground floor doors and windows and dormers opening into upper rooms, proliferated. Arcadelike galleries flanked by *cabinets* graced their rear facades. These were built side-by-side with the taller Creole townhouses, which rose two- to three-stories high. Masonry walls connected these structures, punctuated with narrow passageways and carriage-width driveways that opened into the walled courtyards behind.

ABOVE: The Massons consulted detailed analysis of similar structures to select paint colors for their 1805 Creole cottage, including golden orange stucco and blue-green board-and-batten shutters.

[4] Heard, p. 21.

[5] Toledano, p. 8.

17

The resulting streetscape is the picturesque labyrinth so beautifully described by Heard: "Most of the buildings are hardly perceivable as objects because they cannot be seen in the round. Rather they serve as shapers of space—of the rooms and courtyards within them and of the streets which they confine. . . . The energy lies in the tension between the clear street grid and the idiosyncratic spaces stacked and wedged and hung in interstices behind the streets. Within the thousands of spaces and in the sequences between them reside what might be called the Quarter's myths, myths in the plural because, like the buildings themselves, they have been built up in layers over time, with much lost along the way."[6]

It is no wonder that writers have found fertile ground in New Orleans, where so many nook and niches invite the imagination to linger. Walt Whitman, Sherwood Anderson, William Faulkner, Tennessee Williams, Kate Chopin, and Walker Percy are just of few of America's literary giants who have given tongue to the city's stories. The city also spawned many lesser known but gifted writers who penned impressions of New Orleans and its denizens including Lafcadio Hearn who, during the decade between 1878 and 1888, wrote multiple descriptions that were published in both regional papers and national journals including *Scribner's Magazine*, *The Century Magazine*, and *Harper's Bazaar*.[7]

Born on a Greek Island, raised in Ireland and England, immigrating to America at the age of nineteen, and finding his way as a young journalist from Cincinnati to New Orleans, Hearn was an inveterate wanderer and a keen observer. With an anthropologist's eye and a poet's tongue, he enthusiastically described the city where he found refuge, leaving behind evocative accounts of late nineteenth-century New Orleans before he moved on to find even greater literary success in Japan.

Of the French Quarter, Hearn wrote: "I find much to gratify an artist's eye in this quaint, curious, crooked French Quarter, with its narrow streets and its houses painted in light tints of yellow, green, and sometimes even blue. Neutral tints are common; but there are a great many buildings that can not have been painted for years, and which look neglected and dilapidated as well as antiquated. Solid wooden shutters, painted a bright grass-green, and relieved by walls painted chocolate color, or tinted yellow, have a pretty effect, and suggest many memories of old France."[8]

By the time Hearn settled in New Orleans, the city had grown well beyond the boundaries of the French Quarter. The city's Creole population had spread into new neighborhoods developed from former plantation properties downriver from the Quarter—areas known today by the names Faubourg Marigny and Bywater, as well as a neighborhood

---

[6]Heard, p. 7.

[7]S. Frederick Starr, ed., *Inventing New Orleans: Writings of Lafcadio Hearn* (Jackson, Miss.: University Press of Mississippi, 2001), pp. xiii-xiv.

[8]Lafcadio Hearn, "At the Gate of the Tropics," New Orleans, November 19, 1877, Starr, pp. 6–9.

lake-ward of the Quarter called Faubourg Tremé. Here, the building traditions established in the Quarter continued to find expression in Creole cottages and townhouses, as well as shotguns, narrow houses with rooms aligned from front to back in an *infillade* arrangement. These reflected on their façades the parade of changing styles from Greek Revival and Italianate neoclassicism to late Victorian scrolls and jigsaw work, as well as the craze for cast-iron decoration that flourished in the last half of the nineteenth century.

On the upriver side of the French Quarter, the city's growing Anglo-American population established their own neighborhoods, where townhouse plans imported from London and American northeastern cities proliferated. Row houses sprang up in the early nineteenth century in the American Sector just beyond Canal Street—the division between the Creole and Anglo-American neighborhoods. Julia Row, the largest and best-preserved of these, dating from 1832, reveals the neoclassical styles preferred by the new American residents who flocked to the city following the Louisiana Purchase.

Benjamin H. B. Latrobe, an English-born architect who came to New Orleans from Baltimore in 1819 and died there of yellow fever in 1820, penned his impressions of the city's architecture. He decried the northeastern style row townhouses springing up in New Orleans as inappropriate to the subtropical climate. Instead, he applauded the Creole cottages and townhouses, with their superior cross-ventilation, thick masonry walls, and economical interior floor plans. Although they may not have read Latrobe's comments, the Anglo-Americans soon experienced their justness. By the 1830s, they began expanding into the former plantation lands of Faubourg St. Mary, just upriver from the old city, and gradually into the Garden District and Uptown neighborhoods where they built more commodious homes that were better suited to the climate.

These large, freestanding houses combined English and American floor plans (with side and center hall configurations) with the deep porches associated with Southern architecture and the decorative iron galleries and balconies favored in New Orleans. Their decoration ranged from severe to florid expressions of the Greek Revival, Italianate, and Queen Anne

ABOVE: Many shotguns along Magazine Street have been transformed into shops, including Ann Koerner Antiques.

styles, occasionally veering into the more exotic vocabularies of Gothic, Moorish, Swiss, and later, Romanesque design. Unlike the Creole faubourgs, where gardens were cloistered behind buildings and high masonry walls, the gardens of the Anglo-American neighborhoods spread in front and around their properties, turning each house into a miniature country retreat.

Writing at a time when the Anglo-American parts of the city were experiencing renewed prosperity following the deprivations of the Civil War and ensuing occupation and reconstruction, Hearn documented the architecture and landscape of the Garden District and Uptown neighborhoods.

"The glory of the city is in her Southern homes and gardens," he declared. "One cannot do justice to their beauty. The streets broaden there; the side-paths are bordered with verdant sod as soft and thick as velvet and overshadowed with magnolias; the houses, mostly built in Renaissance style, are embowered in fruit-bearing trees and evergreen gardens, where statues and fountains gleam through thick shrubbery, cunningly trimmed into fantastic forms. . . . And you can walk through this paradise hour after hour, mile after mile; and the air only becomes yet more fragrant and the orange trees more heavily freighted with golden fruit, and the gardens more and more beautiful, as you proceed southwardly. . . ."[9]

Well more than a century after this description was penned, it is still possible to stroll through the upriver neighborhoods and experience this paradisial beauty, even though many mansions fell to the wrecking ball in the mid- to late-twentieth century and large gardens have been subdivided to make room for new buildings. Considering that the city has endured several cycles of boom and bust since these Uptown neighborhoods developed, it is quite astonishing that their appearance and general character is so much intact—particularly considering that so little was done in terms of organized preservation and protective legislation until the last few decades. Long stretches of St. Charles Avenue are still not protected by landmark neighborhood designation, while other parts have been only been protected since 1975 by the Historic District Landmarks Commission.

Ironically, it is in the neighborhood that was first protected by preservation legislation—the Vieux Carré—where the greatest transformation has been wrought, not as much through loss of historic structures but rather changes in urban lifestyles. Although a state constitutional amendment established a Vieux Carré Commission in 1936 with the power to protect the Quarter's buildings from demolition and disfigurement, the unfettered growth of the tourist industry has greatly undermined the texture of community life. The notoriety this quarter gained for boozy, baudy amusements during Prohibition and later World War II, when thirsty soldiers and sailors passed through the city's port of embarkation, endured, surpassing its reputation for architectural interest and the picturesque. Where once residents of Creole

OPPOSITE: One of New Orleans' most prominent turn-of-the-nineteenth-century architects, Thomas Sully, designed this St. Charles Avenue house for himself and his family. Masculine stateliness balanced with whimsical detail characterizes the architect's Queen Anne style residences.

[9]Ibid.

ABOVE: While the Spanish influence rarely appears unalloyed in New Orleans, Patrick Dunne created this pure Spanish fantasy at his Lucullus antiques store in the French Quarter.

cottages and townhouses threw open ground-floor shutters to participate in a lively exchange between domestic and city life, most inhabitants now firmly shutter their houses, barring out the noisy crowds.

A 1936 account of the French Quarter described "[m]any doors . . . shut and clamped and grayed with cobwebs. Half the balconies are begrimed and the iron railings rust-eaten, and humid arches and alleys which characterize the older Franco-Spanish piles of stuccoed brick betray a fatalistic squalor. Yet . . . beauty and the picturesque still linger here, which the blare of radios and smart reconditioning of crumbling façades seem only to emphasize by contrast. . . . [Occasionally] through a chink between some pair of heavy batten window-shutters opened with a reptile wariness, your eye catches a glimpse of lace and brocade upholstery, silver and bronze, and similar rich antiquity."[10]

Today, the buildings of the French Quarter are in far better repair than this description suggests, and the flourishing of fine restaurants—some still in or near their original nineteenth and early twentieth century locations—and elegant antique shops in ground-floor rooms employed as commercial space for more than a century, hearken back to the area's glory days. It is still possible, in early morning or in the lower, less-trafficked blocks of the Quarter, to wander the narrow streets and appreciate the Old World quaintness of an architectural and urban setting that is unique in America and the world. For this, New Orleans' dedicated preservationists can be thanked, as well as for the revitalization and preservation of the neighborhoods spreading both upriver and down from the French Quarter, as well as lake-ward, including Faubourg Tremé, Esplanade Ridge, and Parkview, and across the Mississippi River on Algiers Point.

Many organizations can be credited with preserving these neighborhoods, with so much of their architecture and vestiges of their urban culture intact, including the Friends of the Cabildo, founded in 1956. Not limiting its efforts to preserving the Cabildo and Madame John's Legacy, two of the oldest Spanish colonial buildings in the Louisiana Territory, and sup-

[10]Stanley Clisby Arthur, *Old New Orleans: A History of the Vieux Carré, Its Ancient and Historical Buildings*, quoted in Randolph Delahanty, *Ultimate Guide to New Orleans* (San Francisco: Chronical Books, 1998), p. 113.

porting the Louisiana State Museum, this group also published the New Orleans Architecture series, which details the histories and documents the architecture of many of the city's historic neighborhoods.

In 1957, the Louisiana Landmarks Society was founded to stop the demolition of major landmarks of national and local importance, including the Pitot House. This French colonial style plantation house, c. 1799, was moved to Bayou St. John, restored, and transformed into a house museum. In 1972, the Faubourg Marigny Improvement association was created to draw attention to the massive neglect that threatened the Creole faubourg directly below the French Quarter. This group helped catalyze the creation of other neighborhood-based preservation organizations as well as the establishment of the New Orleans Historic District Landmarks Commission, which allows urban areas of a certain size to create and implement historic districts.

In 1974, the Preservation Resource Center stepped in to add its energies to protecting endangered historic properties and neighborhoods. This organization purchases and renovates properties, works with neighborhood associations, and builds awareness of the power of historic architecture to attract new urban populations, as well as private sector investment, to languishing neighborhoods. The impact of these programs, as well as those of other organizations, can be seen today in the steady reclamation of once threatened neighborhoods and the restoration of their unique and irreplaceable architectural assets.

In the following pages, houses from many of these neighborhoods reveal their hidden charms: the intimate elegance of Creole cottages in Bywater, Faubourg Marigny, and the French Quarter; the stately grandeur of Greek Revival and Italianate mansions in the Garden District; the bold delights of an early twentieth-century house on Algiers Point and a Romanesque Revival mansion on St. Charles Avenue. While some residents revere the past, respecting traditional palettes and perpetuating period styles, others celebrate the present, updating interiors with bright, light colors and contemporary art, reminding us that New Orleans is not a city of dead style, but one that continues to evolve without ever forgetting its roots.

These houses, and the stories of the residents who have shaped them over the last two centuries and who inhabit them today, reveal three fundamental aspects of New Orleans: a sensual passion for the elements—worn brick, crumbling plaster, colorful paint, sinuous iron; a penchant for the eccentric, as demonstrated by a love of masking, parading, and fancy dress balls with elaborate themes and bejeweled pageantry; and insatiable appetite for elegance, whether restrained or utterly exuberant. These collective characteristics, combined with the city's protean nature, at one moment seemingly European, another, Caribbean, and yet another, purely Southern, conspire to create a place of irresistible, evocative charm.

Elemental

NEW ORLEANS

I F NEW ORLEANS HAD ITS OWN PERIODIC TABLE, WITH ELEMENTS ARRANGED FROM THE heaviest to the most ethereal, it might begin with iron, both wrought and cast; granite; marble; limestone; and plaster—smooth or molded into garlands, rosettes, and filigree. Occupying the center of the table would be cypress; bargeboard salvaged from flatboats floated down the Mississippi then dismantled and transformed into the walls of Creole cottages; bales of cotton; bundles of horsehair; and bolts of gleaming silk and satin. The lightest elements would include gold leaf, ashes of roses, bitter chicory, hallucinatory absinthe, and the unfettered fantasy of Mardi Gras floats.

New Orleans also has a language of surface all its own: patina and tarnish; verdigris and varnish; crazed paint, crumbling plaster, and *craqueleur;* waxed wood, whorled glass, worn brick, Welsh slate; distemper and casein. This language tells a story of the alchemical transformation of raw goods into refined objects; the artistry of craftspeople gathered together from Europe, Africa, and the Tropics; the passage of time and effects of heat and light; the pride of generations past; and the careful stewardship of generations present.

While some houses celebrate renewal, with polished surfaces and reproduction fabrics that allow past styles to shine anew, the dwelling places of elemental New Orleans revel in decadence. Rather than stay the hand of time, their owners explore the poignant beauty of genteel decay. They hoard the vestiges of antique paint and plaster as priceless souvenirs of those who died long ago and their domestic impulses. They honor the ingenuity of builders past who knew how to channel light and air to create comfortable living spaces without the benefit of electricity. And they surround themselves with objects and materials that make no effort to hide their age, their nature, or their unspoken histories.

PAGE 24: The Heard house features a traditional gallery/*cabinet* arrangement, with doors opening into small utility rooms that flank the open air porch. The deep blue walls of the porch contrast with the lush greenery of the garden beyond.

OPPOSITE: A late eighteenth-century sideboard and early nineteenth-century hand-blown glass smoke bell illuminated by a single candle create a Vermeer-like setting in Julia Reed's French Quarter dining room. The prints depict the expulsion of Roman Catholic cardinals during Napoleon's captivity of the Pope.

26

From Time to Timelessness

The Home of Kerry Moody

A BYWATER CREOLE COTTAGE

THERE IS A CREOLE COTTAGE ON MONTEGUT STREET THAT SITS FAR BACK FROM THE SIDEWALK, half-seen behind a thick stand of aspidistra and the feathery foliage of old cypress trees. Like most of its neighbors, the one-story cottage probably stood next to the street once, its *abat-vent* (or over-hanging roof) shading the sidewalk beneath. Built in the early 1840s, it may well have been one of many nearby structures that were uprooted and rolled on logs to new locations in the late nineteenth and early twentieth centuries. While the reasons for these relocations were usually practical, reflecting real estate transactions or property improvements, in the case of this house, they also seem poetic, as if the cottage or its owners chose to step back not just from the street, but from time itself, with its relentless insistence upon progress and change.

The cottage stands on what was once the downriver boundary of Faubourg Montegut, one of several neighborhoods settled by upper, middle, and working class Creoles, both black and white, as well as immigrants from Germany, Italy, and Ireland. Now called Bywater, the area is considered to be one of the most intact antebellum neighborhoods in New Orleans.[1] Although many of its pre–Civil War structures received modish ornamentation in the form of decorative jigsaw work and brackets during the late nineteenth century, the basic appearance of the houses, the ethnic and social makeup of their residents, and the quality of life on the streets, which balances residential and commercial demands, has remained much the same for a century and a half.

With no late Victorian decorations obscuring it, the façade of Kerry Moody's house expresses the refined simplicity of the classic Creole cottage. Raised slightly off the ground, the house has four bays including two French doors and two tall windows—all flanked by leaf-green louvered shutters. "This yellow is almost a signature Creole color, not just in New Orleans, but also in France," says Mr. Moody, describing the paint shade he chose for the house's clapboard walls. "It is a golden yellow, almost like sunlight," he adds. "Even when the sun is not shining on the house, it just glows behind the greenery."

OPPOSITE: Mr. Moody selected colors from a traditional Creole palette for his house—warm gold, leaf green, and sky blue beneath the eaves. "The Creoles used a lot of color," explains the designer who has studied Creole architecture in both New Orleans and France.

[1]Toledano, Roulhac, et al, *New Orleans Architecture: The Creole Faubourgs*, vol. IV (Gretna, La., 1974), p. xv.

OPPOSITE: This formal mantel, with fluted pilasters and acanthus leaf scrolls, was a later addition to the house whose three original mantels express the preferred simplicity of Creole design. The mantel holds a collection of early nineteenth-century decanters and a pair of candelabra in the style of Louis XVI.

The interior of the house, also painted a warm shade of yellow, is an equally luminous expression of Creole refinement. Four square rooms of the same size flow easily one to the other in the traditional hall-less floor plan admired by renowned American architect Benjamin H. B. Latrobe in 1819. "These [French-style] one-storied houses are very simple in their plan. The two front rooms open into the street with French glass doors. Those on one side are the dining and drawing rooms, the others, chambers. . . . We derive from the English the habit of desiring that every one of our rooms should be separately accessible and we consider rooms that are thoroughfares as useless. The French and Continental European generally live, I believe, as much to their own satisfaction in their houses as we do in ours and employ the room they have to more advantage because they do not require so much space for passages."[2]

Mr. Moody, whose ancestors include French émigrés hailing from Normandy and Creoles of mixed African and European descent, lives in this dwelling much as his Creole predecessors would have. "I love the energy of this house," he exclaims. "It has a kind of flow that invites you to use all the rooms." In order to enhance the unity among the rooms that open onto one another with glazed French doors, Mr. Moody painted them all the same shade—a color that shifts from bright to burnished gold as the sun passes over the house and sets.

In keeping with the traditional use of rooms, the living and dining rooms occupy one side of the house while the more private, less formal library/sitting room and bedroom make up the second, parallel suite. The kitchen fills the enclosed space at the rear of the house that extends between two original *cabinets*, small utility extensions that today enclose a bathroom and storage closet. But Moody breaks with tradition in his decoration of the house, shying away from the heavy, formal, mahogany furniture and silk upholstery he associates with late eighteenth- and early nineteenth-century Creole cottage décor. "I did not want that," he declares. "I love painted furniture, rustic pieces, and the French provincial style," he adds, revealing his Normandy roots. "I wanted this to look like a country cottage in the heart of the city, but with a touch of sophistication."

Mr. Moody achieved this look by furnishing the cottage with finds from buying trips to France (he is the manager of the New Orleans antiques store Lucullus), antiques discovered at local shops and auctions, and family heirlooms. In the dining room, a pine buffet and tole chandelier sheds light upon a set of painted Louis XVI chairs dressed down with upholstery of period mattress ticking. Above the mantel, early nineteenth-century decanters catch the light, while a Louis XVI mirror with fading mercury-backed glass reflects the glow of candles.

"I find that everybody loves coming into the dining room and the kitchen," says Moody. Although it is not original to the house, the kitchen has a distinctly Old World air, with

---

[2]Benjamin H. B. Latrobe, *Impressions Respecting New Orleans*, edited by Samuel Wilson, Jr. (New York: Columbia University Press, 1951), p. 106; quoted in Toledano, p. 47.

OPPOSITE: Although its provenance cannot be traced, the portrait of a Creole gentleman found in France bears a striking resemblance to Mr. Moody. While the circular ceremonial necklace from Africa displayed beneath the portrait plays tribute to the resident's African ancestry, the fringed slipper chair from France, c. 1800, honors his French roots.

LEFT: Moody discovered the Napoleon III bed on the sidewalks of Paris. The opulence of the velvet-upholstered bed and matching curtains offset the simplicity of the painted plank ceiling and plain plaster walls common to Creole cottages.

its exposed-beam ceiling and terra cotta tile floor. This ambiance is amplified by the selection of French and Louisiana antiques that furnish the room, including a rare cypress *garde-manger* and a marble-topped storage bin from a nineteenth-century French pastry shop. A French bistro table painted bright blue adds a spot of color, while a stainless steel Viking range interjects a modern note.

Every piece of furniture in the cottage tells a story, whether the Napoleon III bed Mr. Moody found for sale on a Paris sidewalk or a spherical ornament made of ebony and ivory discovered at a local flea market and now displayed in the library. But the story the collector loves to tell most is the one about the painting that almost got away. Hanging over the living room mantel, this c. 1840 portrait by an unknown artist depicts an elegant light-skinned Creole gentleman in formal attire who bears a striking resemblance to Mr. Moody. The collector first encountered the painting in a Normandy antique shop nearly a decade ago. "It really captured my imagination, but I could not afford to buy it at the time," he recalls.

ABOVE: A collection of beads from the French and Irish coasts—some made of melted Coke bottles—hangs from the corner of a painted wood mantel.

OPPOSITE: The kitchen is furnished with a marble-topped storage bin from a nineteenth-century French pastry shop and a Louisiana *garde-manger* made from cypress.

The years passed and the portrait continued to haunt him, even more intensely once Mr. Moody bought the c. 1840 Creole cottage that provided a perfect setting. On a buying trip in Paris six or seven years after he left the portrait behind, he strolled through the Flea Market and encountered some old colleagues—the same antique dealers who had relocated from Normandy to Paris. His heart racing, Mr. Moody followed them back to their stall where he spotted the painting, hanging high on the wall. Incredulous that fate had granted him a second chance, he bought the painting and brought it home to hang in place of pride in his living room.

"There's something about this painting," Mr. Moody muses. "It just seems like I was meant to have it, that it was meant to hang here." Whether or not the portrait actually does depict the resident's long-lost ancestor, which is quite possible, it completes the Creole essence that imbues this cottage with the burnished aura of a place that has stepped out of time into timelessness.

34

Floating Island

The Home of Julia Reed and John Pearce

A FRENCH QUARTER DEPENDENCY

ON THE GROUND FLOOR OF JULIA REED AND JOHN PEARCE'S FRENCH QUARTER HOME, the light has a subaqueous quality lent by the reflections of sunbeams flickering on tropical foliage in courtyard gardens. Built as an ancillary building, with kitchen and storage areas below and living quarters above, the house is cloven on the ground floor by an arched breezeway that connects the main courtyard of the property to a smaller one behind. The two ground-floor structures join on the second floor to create a loftlike space where the light is gossamer and bright. This unusual dependency rises behind a fine Creole cottage, built c. 1810 by a prosperous merchant or planter, which turns a red stucco façade to bustling Bourbon Street.

Vacant for several years during the French Quarter's mid-twentieth-century nadir, when prosperous residents flocked to outlying semiurban and suburban neighborhoods, the property was rescued by appreciative new owners in 1963. "The minute we saw this house, it spoke to us," recalls Betty DeCell, who purchased the house with her husband, architect John E. DeCell. Mr. DeCell renovated the two houses, transforming the front cottage into three apartments and turning the back house into a home for his young wife and new baby. When they bought the property, an old privy still stood in the yard where a stand of banana trees now thrives and masses of *Rose Montana* formed a living canopy over the courtyard between the two houses.

"Being in that little back house was like being on an island," reminisces Mrs. DeCell, who now lives in a nineteenth-century townhouse on Esplanade Avenue. "You're right in the middle of the city, but with the walls and courtyards, you have a sense of detachment. Nobody knows the house is there unless you invite them in." Famous guests have included writers Sherwood Anderson, who rented the back house in the 1925, and William Faulkner, a friend of Anderson's rumored to have been uninvited during a particularly inebriated visit. The house's current resident, journalist and author Julia Reed, counts herself very fortunate to have found the hidden house and its secret garden.

OPPOSITE: A typical Creole color scheme of deep red walls with cool green details is employed throughout the property. A breezeway bisects the ground floor of the dependency, terminating in a tiny courtyard that is just the right size for plein-air dining.

Although she grew up on what she describes as "six idyllic acres in the Mississippi Delta surrounded by ancient live oaks and pecan trees with a mother who is practically the Bird Woman of Alcatraz," Ms. Reed found her way as an adult to New York City. "I spent a decade in the city without even a fire escape to put a flower pot, so I was very happy to find what passes for me as a great nature preserve here!" she exclaims. Ms. Reed began visiting New Orleans in 1991 when she covered Edwin Edwards' sensational race for the Louisiana governorship against David Duke. She then secured a contract to write a book of essays about the South entitled *Queen of the Turtle Derby and Other Subjects*, and ultimately married New Orleans attorney John Pearce, deepening her ties to the city.

Ms. Reed, who still keeps an apartment in New York, decided to rent the DeCells' back house the minute she saw the courtyards. "It's easy to be a gardener in a courtyard, because it's like a terrarium," she says. Parterres and large terra-cotta containers scattered around the main courtyard's mossy paving stones hold citrus trees—navel and Satsuma oranges, Key limes, and Meyer lemons; a bay tree; a gardenia bush; and flowering vines poetically named *fleurs d'amour* and *yesterday, today, and tomorrow*. In the back courtyard, the resident tamed an overgrown stand of bamboo into a living wall that towers above a marble-topped wrought-iron table surrounded by French bistro chairs. "That's my real dining room for nine months out of the year," she comments.

"When I have a big party," says Ms. Reed, who writes about food and entertaining for the *New York Times Magazine* and *Food & Wine*, among other publications, "the house is open, and the front and back courtyards become rooms. I put tables and a piano out in the main courtyard." One of the things the current resident loves most

Architect Jack DeCell installed a graceful circular staircase connecting the ground floor with this second-floor living area and the attic above. Originally, access to the second-floor living quarters was provided by the exterior staircase on the front of the building.

about the house is the way the indoor and outdoor spaces flow together. "There's not a room that doesn't open to the outside. It really does feel like you're living outside half the time."

Ms. Reed has great admiration for the quality of Mr. DeCell's renovation of the old building. "Jack had not only good taste," she says, "but a lot of restraint, which is the same thing." While the kitchen and storage rooms originally had only shutters on their outside openings, mismatched doors and windows were added at a later date. Mr. DeCell kept these, as well as the simple Creole-style cypress mantels on the second floor, from which he stripped layers of paint. He removed partitions that separated the second floor into three small rooms, installing a small bathroom and storage cupboard in the center of the space, which effectively divides it into two interconnected rooms. He also replaced a ship's ladder with a spiral staircase to provide easy access between the floors without taking up much room.

Ms. Reed uses the loft area that floats above the courtyards as a sitting room and bedroom, while the ground-floor rooms on one side of the breezeway serve as dining room and kitchen and, on the far side, as a remarkably airy writing office. "There are two French doors in my office, and when both are open, it's like a wind tunnel," remarks the writer. With a cement floor painted white, white-washed plaster walls, and a white-painted open-beam ceiling, the office provides a luminous backdrop for Ms. Reed's collection of antique furniture, prints, and books.

"Basically, the book situation is out of hand," Ms. Reed laughs, pointing to stacks of books atop an English, nineteenth-century secretary that belonged to her grandmother, a French tilt-top, wine-tasting table, and a large trestle table that serves as her desk. The volumes range from frequently consulted reference books to favorite collections of poetry and novels by Southern authors. Maps of the surrounding area hang on the walls, including one of Louisiana and Mississippi that Ms. Reed found in Prague. This hangs below the taxidermied head of a wild boar—a gift from the owner of a French Quarter shop.

ABOVE: A sampling of the owner's favorite things, including books of poetry, birds' nests, and shells.

OPPOSITE: A secretary bookcase holds a collection of old cookbooks. A French wine-tasting table and an antique *campeche* chair round out an eclectic selection of furniture in the writer's ground-floor office.

41

"I've always loved the more bizarre animate things," confesses Ms. Reed, who collects nests, shells, horns, objects made from horn, and bird prints, including an antique print depicting the Great Butcher Bird, a small predator known for impaling and decapitating its prey. The mix of English, French, and American antiques; colonial style furnishings including a *campeche* chair and *verre eglomisé* portraits of Indian officers from the time of the Raj; African details including textiles from Kenya; and likenesses and specimens of local fauna reminds Ms. Reed of what she calls "the roots of the eclectic history of New Orleans."

Mrs. DeCell, who is a frequent guest in her old home, admires Ms. Reed's manner of occupying the house. "She lives in it just right, not gussied up or fussed up, but very elegantly, in an understated way that befits the house," she says. "Julia is a visual person, a literary person, a culinary person. She really responds to the house and that makes me happy." Ms. Reed confirms her landlady's sentiments. "I'm so spoiled," she says. "I don't know what I'm going to do when I have to depart from this place."

LEFT: **Jack DeCell chose a plain mantel of unstained pine as an appropriately simple element for the former slave quarters. A print of a Great Butcher Bird is one among several antique ornithological prints in the room.**

42

House of Good Fortune

The Home of Mary Cooper and Tomio Thomann

A BYWATER CREOLE TOWNHOUSE

MARY COOPER, A CHAIR-CANER AND COLORIST FROM NEW ORLEANS, CONSIDERS HERSELF VERY fortunate to be the owner and restorer of an early-nineteenth-century Creole townhouse in the Bywater neighborhood downriver from Faubourg Marigny. Her partner, artist Tomio Thomann, whose roots spread from Bywater to his birthplace in Okinawa, agrees. "We just get luckier and luckier," he says. Upon viewing the before and after pictures of the house they have spent more than a year restoring, it becomes evident that good fortune, supplemented by fortitude, the generosity of friends, and a fine eye for beauty, has indeed played a role in this remarkable transformation.

When Cooper's daughter Jennifer acquired the house in 2000, the derelict building revealed both structural damage inflicted by termites and moisture and aesthetic depravities wreaked by previous residents. Although a significant portion of its original material had been removed or decayed beyond repair, the basic floor-plan of the eight-room townhouse remained intact. A nineteenth-century kitchen and laundry structure had been moved forward from the back of the large lot and attached to the townhouse, creating a spacious—if slightly eccentric— flow of rooms and a large back lot. Although the property had a lot of potential, the younger Ms. Cooper eventually gave up on the restoration and sold the house to her mother, an experienced preservationist.

Joined by Thomann, who counts carpentry among his many skills, Cooper took over the project with enthusiasm. She rejoiced at each discovery of original material: rosehead nails indicating the house is older than its earliest known documentation from the year 1840 suggests; an original cypress door sandwiched between two walls; and splattered paint on old floorboards that provided a historically based palette for the interior. "When we removed the dropped ceiling in the parlor, we even found the old picture nails still in the walls," Cooper gleefully notes.

OPPOSITE: A typical Creole townhouse, this structure was designed with no interior halls and an open side passageway to provide access to the rear *gallerie/cabinets* and garden.

The couple also delighted in hunting down replacement material for missing elements. "Some friends called one day to say they had old roof sheathing that they thought we could use to replace missing bargeboard," recalls Thomann, pointing to the rough, wide vertical planks forming the walls of the first floor bathroom. Another friend telephoned to say he just saw someone throw pieces of an old mantel from a truck. Cooper rushed to the scene to find fragments of an antique Creole mantel with tapered cigar-shaped columns that will soon grace the parlor. "Just like Cinderella's shoe, it fits perfectly," she marvels.

Like most Creole townhouses, the house has no grand front entrance. While box steps would once have led to French doors opening into the front rooms, most visitors would have entered by walking along the outside of the house and coming through the back. "The Creoles used the front entrance for funerals and 'fancy' visitors, never family," Cooper explains. Today, the house's main entrance is a side door that opens into the dining room that was created in the late nineteenth century, when the kitchen house was joined to the main structure.

Rather than mask the fact that the walls on either side of the room were once exterior surfaces, the couple accentuated this history by sheathing them with weatherboard and restoring original window openings with board-and-batten shutters. "It's sort of an indoor-outdoor dining room," says Cooper, who asked a friend to make a long table for it. The base of the table, with blocky chamfered legs carved from antique cypress, is a reproduction of a table from the Ursuline Convent. The cypress top is one of the couple's garage sale finds.

A window that opens into the kitchen can be closed with the shutter that is usually left ajar to enhance the flow of air and light and expose the sill, where seasonal fruits and vegetables sit to ripen. A collection of enamel cookware pops ripe tomato red against the kitchen's dark turquoise walls—an original color. A ceiling fan whirs throughout the summer months (the house has no central heat or air-conditioning) and a tall door painted ochre opens onto the gallery, which maintains its original configuration of a deep porch, bracketed by two *cabinets*, or little rooms, one which now serves as a storage room, the other, as a laundry.

ABOVE: **A long porcelain-coated iron sink extends along one kitchen wall.**

OPPOSITE: **A large window opens into the kitchen where an original color scheme provides a cool setting.**

46

RIGHT: Fifty-year-old
toile with a dusky chartreuse
background inspired
the color scheme of the
summer bedroom, which
is furnished with
Louisiana-made antique
furniture of cypress.

The residents use the gallery, which is floored with teak they located through a newspaper advertisement, as an outdoor living room. It overlooks an area they transformed into a traditional Creole parterre garden by moving a collection of huge flagstones to define a grid with four beds. A Satsuma orange tree stands in the middle of each parterre, surrounded by nasturtiums, lilies, pansies, roses (including a Duchesse du Brabant and a Louis Philippe offered by friends), and artichokes. "It's a farm, really, not a garden," says Cooper, a skilled gardener who enjoys mixing edible and ornamental plants. She also makes liqueurs from the garden's citrus crop, including limoncello, which inspired the house's striking exterior shade.

One of the most enclosed rooms in the house is a space opening off the dining room which Cooper calls "the little green room." Diminutive furniture graces this intimate sitting area, including a Louisiana child's armoire, c. 1810–20, made of cherry and poplar, with Fiche hinges and pressed brass escutcheons. "All of my antique dealer friends like to visit that piece," Cooper laughs, explaining that antique children's furniture is quite rare. The room also includes a small American daybed faux-grained to resemble rosewood. A pair of American classical chairs, also surfaced with rosewood faux-bois, is upholstered with remnants of vintage toile.

LEFT: Unfinished wooden floorboards and a sky-blue ceiling give the guest room the breezy aura of a summer porch while wrought-iron furnishings, including an ancient blacksmith-made curtain rod, lend a monastic severity.

ABOVE: Rescued weather-board of rough cypress covers the walls of the small sitting room that connects the guest bed-room to the bath. Vintage linen tea towels curtain antique doors that bear the scars of original ram's-horn hinges.

Upstairs, the ceiling and moldings of the summer bedroom are painted chartreuse to match another piece of vintage toile that curtains a pair of French doors. Louisiana-made antiques of cypress furnish the room, their dark wood contrasting handsomely with the white walls. The simple lines of the triangular headboard and a pyramidal chest evoke the dignity and mystery of Egyptian temples—a trait shared by much of Louisiana-made furniture, which reveals a severe economy of design.

The balcony spanning the front of the house connects the summer bedroom to a guestroom that has an entirely different aura. Pale gray walls, plain white gauze curtains, and iron furnishings lend the room a monastic air. Indeed, the nineteenth-century wrought-iron beds may have been made for a religious (or possibly, a military) order. Certainly, the wrought-iron cross hanging on the wall once graced religious surroundings. A pair of hand-wrought andirons standing in the naked brick fireplace (all but one of the original mantels had disappeared) echoes the shapes of the cross. Tiny caned children's chairs sit on either side of a tall

Louisiana armoire with a *gros-rouge* finish made by rubbing brick dust or bull's blood into the wood.

This airy retreat promises to catch cool breezes throughout the steamy summer. The French doors offer two layers of protection from, or invitation to, the outdoor elements: exterior doors with louvered shutters and interior doors with glazed mullions. When open, the doors offer access to the narrow balcony overlooking a typically modest streetscape of Bywater, one of New Orleans' most ethnically and sociologically diverse neighborhoods for two centuries. When the doors and shutters are closed, the room becomes a quiet cloister. From the ethereal tones of this second-floor retreat to the vibrant colors employed in other rooms, the walls of the house seem to express a quiet joy at having found such attentive and appreciative inhabitants.

A Measure of Grace

The Home of Ann and Frank Masson

A FRENCH QUARTER CREOLE COTTAGE

ALL TOO OFTEN, EFFORTS TO IMITATE THE PAST WITH HISTORICALLY INSPIRED FAÇADES, reproduction fabrics and furniture, and commercially marketed period paint palettes, fall short of the mark, offering only uncomfortably self-conscious imitations of the past while obscuring irreplaceable vestiges of historic reality. More satisfying restorations establish new and meaningful bonds with the past through a kind of channeling, a near supernatural communication with long gone people and their daily life through the physical medium of the plastic arts. Approached in this way, iron, brick, plaster, pigment, and wood can be coaxed to connect the restorer to the past with which he or she wishes to commune.

This is the manner in which Ann and Frank Masson, an architectural historian and a historically informed architect, respectively, treated their restoration of Dolliole Cottage, a French Quarter dwelling described in William Mitchell's *Classic New Orleans* as "a perfect archetypal Creole cottage."[1] The house is named for its builder, Jean Louis Dolliole, the son of a Frenchman who arrived in New Orleans during the Spanish period and formed a permanent liaison with a free woman of color. A prominent builder and successful real estate entrepreneur in the French Quarter and Tremé neighborhoods, Jean Louis Dolliole built this cottage in 1805 as a residence for himself and his wife, Hortense.

The Massons discovered the diminutive house in 1979. Having been uninhabited since 1952, following the departure of two Creole ladies who had lived in it sans plumbing, electricity, or inside kitchen, the house offered virgin ground for restoration. The floor was completely rotted out, much of the interior woodwork deteriorated, and the brick structure impregnated with moisture—but unlike many other antique buildings in the French Quarter, the cottage was almost untouched by modern hands.

[1]William R. Mitchell, Jr., *Classic New Orleans* (New Orleans and Savannah: Martin-St. Martin Publishing Company, 1993), p. 68.

OPPOSITE: Built by a prominent free man of color, builder and entrepreneur Jean Louis Dolliole, this 1805 Creole cottage exhibits the hallmarks of this regional type, which evolved from small urban dwellings in France and the French West Indies.

55

ABOVE: A portrait of
Mrs. Masson's Maryland
ancestor Mary Green Todd
graces the dining room.

OPPOSITE: A copy of an
eighteenth-century
Flemish harpsichord
evokes the simple elegance
of Vermeer's interiors.

Mrs. Masson admits that the initial appearance of the house, which she describes as a "ruined shell," was daunting. The couple's real estate agent reportedly gasped when they asked her to draw up a contract, and many friends admitted that they had also toured the cottage and given it up as unsalvageable. But the Massons bought it and began a year-long restoration during which they made a few concessions to the modern age, adding electricity, plumbing, and an indoor kitchen, while demonstrating a rigorous commitment to re-creating surfaces and details using traditional materials and methods of craftsmanship. According to a 1999 article in *British Homes and Gardens*, "their quest for authenticity was so effective that it fueled gossip and speculation all around the French Quarter . . . ," including a rumor that they lived without electricity.

Fortunately, sufficient vestiges of the interior moldings and iron hardware remained to enable a retinue of contemporary craftsmen to replicate missing materials. Photographs taken of the house during the 1930s by noted New Orleans restoration architect Richard Koch and by Frances Benjamin Johnston for the Carnegie Survey of Southern Historic Architecture also helped the couple discover details about the house's early nineteenth-century appearance. To these sources of information, the Massons contributed their own considerable knowledge of New Orleans' architectural and decorative traditions.

After repairing the brick walls, they hired members of the Vandergriff family firm to apply interior plaster employing the early nineteenth-century method. Because the house was built of locally made brick that is softer and more water-permeable than other types, it required a treatment that foregoes the usual moisture barrier. Three-coat plaster made from lime and sand with a small amount of cement was applied to the walls. Mrs. Masson described the surface, which is susceptible to rising damp and requires repairs every five years, for an article in a local magazine: "Now the walls are starting to look truly antique, with layers of patches and irregular stains that come and go with the weather."[2]

[2]Bonnie Warren, "Rooms with a Vieux," *Louisiana Life*, Winter 1997–98, n.p.

ABOVE: Because the original mantels had been replaced in the 1830s, Frank Masson designed new mantels appropriate to the date and style of the house.

Although the house offered few clues regarding its original palette, the Massons studied paint analysis from other Creole structures of the period to arrive at the color scheme. The exterior is painted a warm golden orange with board-and-batten shutters in a contrasting shade of blue-green. Varying tones of gray characterize the steeply pitched roof covered in slate with copper coping. The Massons had hoped to restore the roof with barrel tiles, a popular early nineteenth-century material in New Orleans, but the structure could no longer support this heavier roof.

58

In addition to its materials and colors, the façade of the house demonstrates several other quintessential aspects of early Creole cottages. Unlike later ones, which often feature dormer windows offering light and ventilation to a second level of bedrooms, this cottage has an unbroken roof. A copper-sheathed extension known as an *abat-vent* reaches out from the roof over the sidewalk, protecting the house from sunlight and rain while also shielding pedestrians. This typical detail intrigued Baltimore-based architect Benjamin H. B. Latrobe when he came to New Orleans in 1819. "It has a very great advantage both with regard to the interior of the dwelling and to the street," he wrote.

All four of the house's ground-level rooms open to the outside with glazed French doors and windows, each equipped with strap-hinge shutters that can be thrown open or bolted shut with wrought-iron latches and hooks. While some of this hardware is original, missing pieces were replicated by Donald Streeter, a nationally known restoration blacksmith from New Jersey who has since retired. "The sound of all that wrought iron snapping into place is very comforting and gives me great pleasure to think about the blacksmiths, both in 1805 and 1981, who made the hardware," Mr. Masson told an interviewer.[3]

The rear of the house still boasts its original open loggia and *cabinets*, small storage rooms that today house a bathroom on one side and a laundry room on the other. Other than these modern amenities, the house appears much as it did when constructed by Jean Louis Dolliole. Mrs. Dolliole's posthumous inventory of possessions served as another touchstone for the Massons as they furnished their house. Although Mrs. Masson describes the décor as "a little too Americanized," the furnishings and decorative objects, many family heirlooms, date mostly from the early nineteenth century. Research using newspaper reports from the period, however, assured the historian that "much of the furniture coming into New Orleans in the first decade of the nineteenth century was coming directly from the northeast, with only a limited amount from France."

"Although vernacular builders, many, like Dolliole, achieved a measure of grace and refinement in their buildings," Mr. Masson notes. Both in its graceful appearance and the amazing grace of its salvation by the Massons, this cottage is an example of the miraculous resuscitation of the past that can be achieved by thoughtful, thorough preservationists. "This house is living proof that nothing is ever too far gone," Mrs. Masson declares.

---

[3]Ibid.

BELOW: An antiques dealer and friend discovered this nineteenth-century beadwork rendering of a home owned by "C. Masson" in 1834. The Chinese cloisonné lamp was given to Mrs. Masson's grandmother by a well-traveled friend in the 1920s.

Creole Alchemy

The Heard House

A BYWATER CREOLE COTTAGE

"[A]N ALCHEMY OF CAREFUL BUILDING, WEATHER, TIME AND A HISTORY OF THOUGHTFUL human habitation"—these are the elements to which architect and author Malcolm Heard ascribes the sensual integrity of the French Quarter.[1] He might easily have applied the same words to the Creole cottage he and his family restored twenty-five years ago and continue to inhabit in nearby Bywater. Fascinated by the evolution of house types and building styles in his adopted city, the native Mississippian was intrigued by the architectural puzzles presented by the house he purchased in 1977.

According to research conducted by Heard's wife, Alicia Rogan, the house was built in the 1850s by a man named Pierre Sévère Wiltz. "His name combines two French names with a German one, showing right away the mingling of cultures that are typical in New Orleans," notes Mrs. Heard. The house Wiltz built reveals another marriage of two cultures—Creole and American. "If it didn't have a center hall, it would have the typical floor plan of the Creole cottage," Mrs. Heard explains, indicating the four ground-floor rooms, the half-story with dormers above, and the pair of *cabinets*, or storage closets, flanking a gallery at the rear. But the center hall, albeit more narrow and less ornamental than those traditionally employed in American houses, reveals the growing assimilation of the design idea by New Orleans' Creole residents in the mid-nineteenth century.

Although the house suffered from neglect and had been remodeled during the Victorian and Depression periods, little had been done that was irreversible. Many of the materials that had been removed, including louvered and battened shutters, still remained on the property. "There were sheds within sheds behind the house," Mrs. Heard recalls, including one made entirely from the old shutters. These were reattached to the house, restoring a typical element of the Creole cottage's exterior.

[1] Malcolm Heard, *The French Quarter Manual* (Tulane School of Architecture, New Orleans, 1997), p. 143.

60

Though Hurricane Betsy had blown off the four chimneys and much of the original slate roofing material in 1965, the exterior walls, made from planks salvaged from Mississippi River flatboats and covered with weatherboard, were structurally sound. Within, much of the interior plaster was intact and the six mantels remained.

"Our goal was to keep as much original material intact as possible," explains Mrs. Heard, who took responsibility for selecting paint colors and planting the large garden while her husband planned the architectural restoration project that occurred in stages. The last of these was completed just a few years ago, when Mr. Heard redesigned the two *cabinets* at the rear of the house to accommodate a bathroom on one side and a kitchen on the other. While maintaining the overall spirit of the *cabinets*—utilitarian extensions that originally flanked an open-air gallery—the architect injected sleeker modern notes through the use of contemporary fixtures and finishes.

During this renovation, the enclosed gallery was reopened to the exterior, but in a surprising way. One of the aspects Mr. Heard admired most about Creole architecture was "the wonderfully subtle gradations between inside and outside established by its traditional devices of dealing with the climate."[2] Mr. Heard's solution to shaping a space that would address the back garden but still provide privacy and security was to create a wall of shutters that could be thrown open or pull closed and locked. With stationary louvers, the shutters allow light and air to flow into the gallery even when shut, providing ventilation for the three rooms— kitchen, dining room, and guest room—and the hallway that opens onto it.

Mr. Heard also redesigned the front door to include a pair of panels that open, bringing air and light into the hall from the street side of the house. The architect took

---

[2]Heard, p. 41.

PREVIOUS PAGE: Originally, this Creole cottage had four French doors opening directly onto the sidewalk. Although these doors were transformed into casement windows in the late nineteenth century, the full-length board and batten shutters are reminders of their original shape. The roofs of the dormers are covered with Welsh slate—a material that once covered the entire roof.

OPPOSITE: The dining room's original fenestration remains intact, with a French door opening onto the surrounding yard. Openings on all four sides of the room encourage cross-ventilation, while the fireplace offers warmth in the brief winter season.

OPPOSITE: The gallery's slim columns and balustrade were shifted slightly toward the house in order to accommodate floor-to-ceiling louvered shutters that close flush to the gallery, creating a space that offers security and privacy as well as natural light and ventilation.

LEFT: The Golden section inspired the proportions of the rhythmic grid of positive and negative space that divides the rear wall of the kitchen.

an even more playful approach to opening the kitchen's rear wall, which he pierced with a window fitted with retractable panels of glass and screen. With both panels open, the window provides an unobstructed aperture into the backyard, framing a cropped view of camellias, magnolias, and banana trees and ushering in seasonal scents and sounds.

Painted white with intense blue shutters and crowned with a shining roof of standing seam metal, the house has a pristine, almost ethereal appearance from without. Within, a richer palette reigns, with rooms painted sun-warmed tones of gold and burnt red and a vibrant green hall running like a shaded allée down its center. When the Heards' professional painter refused to paint the hall, insisting the antique plaster was too fragile to hold an even coat, the couple took on the project with a pair of friends who co-owned the house with them at the time. Rather than obscure the variegated green surface, they enhanced it with a sheer green wash that modulated its tones and textures. "People used to come over and say either, 'Oh, how beautiful,' or 'Oh, this hall has a lot of potential,'" Mrs. Heard laughs.

The rooms are sparely furnished with Southern antiques whose dark finish and large proportions add ballast to the high-ceiling spaces. No curtains hang from the windows, which all have exterior shutters to control the flow of light and air. Each of the ground floor rooms has French windows that open into the surrounding yard. Originally, the front rooms also had French windows opening onto the sidewalk, but these were turned into casement windows in the late nineteenth century, when the lower portions were severed from the upper, glazed parts, and sealed shut.

"We loved the proportions of the house, the way the spaces flow, and how the house opens up to the outside," says Mrs. Heard. In choosing paint colors, she had to take this flow into consideration, since each ground floor room is visible from the next, and all can be seen from the hall. Also, the shutters are visible from within each room, which is one reason why Mrs. Heard chose a blue not distant from the hue of a summer sky. Ultimately, she chose the same shade of blue for the shuttered gallery behind the house, although this was not her original choice.

"We had the idea that the walls, the ceilings, and the shutters should all be painted the same color," she recalls. At first, the Heards thought that color should be green, to link the transitional space to the lush tropical garden beyond. But then they decided that it should be blue to provide contrast with the garden's verdant foliage. The ultramarine shade they chose, which Mrs. Heard describes as blue-blue-blue, creates an intense glow of its own. At once traditional and contemporary in its appearance, the gallery provides the perfect bridge linking not only the interior to the surrounding landscape, but also uniting the nineteenth-century aspects of the house to its twenty-first century manifestation.

OPPOSITE: A love for the arts and crafts runs through Mrs. Heard's family, whose mother and aunt both attended Sophie Newcomb's famous art school. The painting over the bed was made by Xavier Gonzalez, who taught Mrs. Heard's aunt at Newcomb in the 1930s.

Beauty Bared

The Home of Mae Fern Schroeder & Christopher Edwards

AN UPTOWN CREOLE TOWNHOUSE

A RIDE ON THE ST. CHARLES AVENUE STREET CAR MIGHT LEAD TO THE ASSUMPTION THAT THE nineteenth-century architecture of the Uptown district is uniformly large, ostentatious, and Anglo-American in its purposeful rejection of Creole influence upon both floor plan and decoration. But a double Creole townhouse located on Delachaise Street, just a block and a half above the majestic boulevard, belies this generalization, revealing the French roots of the land upon which this American suburb grew. Although the present owner can find no record of when the house was built, her research reveals that the property was owned by a dizzying succession of white and black Creoles in the first six decades of the nineteenth century, including members of the Delachaise and Livaudais plantation aristocracies.

"The Anglos moved in and surrounded them," explains Mae Fern Schroeder, who has pored over archives in an effort to untangle the mysteries presented by the house. While the floor plan has much in common with that of classic Creole townhouses, the decoration of the façade is a puzzling combination of French and American influences. Built of brick fired at the Delachaise brickyard and surfaced with tinted stucco, the house's building materials are traditionally Creole, but the double gallery supported by Doric pillars bears close resemblance to the Greek revival edifices constructed by mid-nineteenth-century Anglo-Americans.

Yet little of this was visible when Ms. Schroeder and her husband Chris Edwards first saw the house while bicycling in the neighborhood. "It was so enshrouded with trees that you could barely see it from a car," she recalls. "I don't think many people even knew it was there." On the lookout for a real estate bargain, the couple quickly made an offer on the house, which, with its air of genteel decay, appealed to the couple's romantic fascination with the South. But once she and Mr. Edwards moved in and began restoration, they felt overwhelmed.

"It's such a huge house, and so confusing," says Ms. Schroeder. "I don't even know how many rooms we have." Part of the confusion stems from the fact that the house had originally been constructed as a duplex, with a pair of joined two-story residences facing the street and a two-story service structure in the rear. Over time, the house was subdivided into a

OPPOSITE: While the layout of this duplex townhouse conforms to the hall-less Creole plan, with two parallel suites of rooms flowing in an *infillade* arrangement from front to back, the appearance of the façade reflects the Greek Revival style popular among the Uptown area's Anglo-American residents.

OPPOSITE: Both sides of the house have spacious front parlors that open through glazed French doors with louvered shutters onto the gallery, providing maximum control of air and light.

warren of rooms. Openings were made to connect rooms that did not formerly communicate and partitions were added to divide parts of the house into discrete apartments. "We tried to bring it back as much as possible to the original floor plan," says Ms. Schroeder, who now lives in one half of the duplex with her husband, renting the other half to tenants.

The couple also worked to restore the house to its original appearance, removing layers of twentieth-century surfaces to reveal antique plaster and wood. In some rooms, the old walls lay hidden behind cheap paneling; in others, more stubborn surfaces required removal. "The dining room was heinous," exclaims Ms. Schroeder, describing "joint compound rolled on to look like meringue" and cornice molding decorated with a pattern of spades and clubs applied in shades of orange and Kelly green. The couple stripped the molding, leaving it bare, and scraped the joint compound off the walls, revealing plaster with marble-like vestiges of rose and coral paint, which they retained.

Unfortunately, the plaster in the front parlors had been replaced with sheetrock and the mantels had been removed. Here, the couple created the illusion of historical trappings by constructing new mantels modeled on extant ones in other rooms and recreating traditional surfaces. They removed the decades-old sheetrock, plastering the walls with a modern technique, sans horsehair, and replaced missing floorboards with similar material, finishing them with linseed oil and wax. "This is the way wood floors were treated, before the days of polyurethane," says Mr. Edwards. They coated the ceilings with paint made from distemper in a casein base, a mixture sold by an Australian company named Porter's Original Paints specializing in historically based mediums and colors. For the walls, they chose oil-based paint to which they added ochre-colored dry pigment to increase the depth of hue. They applied the paint with brushes instead of rollers for a more historically accurate and sensually appealing surface.

Although they weren't exactly faithful to the original colors of the rooms, Ms. Schroeder and Mr. Edwards used a palette inspired by paint traces they found on original surfaces. Wherever possible, the couple reused materials and fittings that remained in the house. "We were fortunate that so many of the original fittings were intact," notes Mr. Edwards. They even saved floorboards and wall studs that were too damaged for architectural use, transforming them into a rustic table that fills the narrow, rectangular dining room. The couple also made frequent trips to salvage yards and antique markets during the restoration, searching for old doorknobs and escutcheons.

In decorating the rooms, which range from the grandly proportioned double parlors to the intimate chambers of the original service building, Ms. Schroeder opted for a style that marries minimalism and romanticism. "Although the house is pretty grand, it isn't fancy," she says. Taking cues from this, she chose single, large pieces of furniture as dominant notes in each room. A grand piano nearly fills the front parlor, its ivory keyboard, open top, and horsehair

The mantel in the second parlor is a copy of an extant one found on the other side of the duplex house. Tall doors with transoms lead from the second parlor to the dining room and to the stair hall beyond, enhancing cross-ventilation.

74

stool providing a series of surfaces upon which the sun plays as it makes its swing around the house. A nine-foot long bench salvaged from a nineteenth-century railroad station runs the length of one wall in the second parlor. With their typical attention to period detail, the couple upholstered the bench with horsehair and cotton stuffing, hand-tying 200 knots, and covering it with antique, hand-woven linen.

Ms. Schroeder welded decorative elements of copper and brass to create lights for the parlors reminiscent of European garden chandeliers, stringing them with opalescent beads made in Holland in the early eighteenth century. A pair of lanterns from an Alabama plantation hangs in the stair hall at the rear of the house, adding an elegant note to the hauntingly decadent space. "How to be true to the house . . . that was always our mantra," Ms. Schroeder muses. "Now I walk through the house and say, 'Oh, I can't believe we live here.' It's such a beautiful home."

In addition to unleashing the haunting beauty of their house's rooms, Ms. Schroeder and Mr. Edwards also lavished attention upon their garden, creating an oasis in the midst of the city's urban chaos. "Our tiny pond is full of goldfish and catfish, tadpoles, and darner naiads, which look like stout dragonflies," says Ms. Schroeder. "We have butterflies, skinks, anoles, frogs, toads, and lizards, and the occasional marauding egret. During parts of the year, the frogs and toads sing all night. Even in the winter, we enjoy our crops of blood oranges; satsumas; Key limes; Meyer, Seville, and variegated pink lemons. This is the life."

OPPOSITE: The delicate serpentine handrail of the staircase is still intact. Plantation lanterns from Alabama with etched glass globes illuminate the stair hall.

ABOVE LEFT: The original mantel in the guest room shows signs that it was altered to accommodate a coal burning stove at a later date.

ABOVE RIGHT: A *modiste's* model from Paris stands sentry in a guest room.

77

Salvaged Beauty

The Home of Barbara and Jeffrey Griffin

A LOWER GARDEN DISTRICT CENTER HALL COTTAGE

CONSTRUCTED IN 1837 FOR WILLIAM GOODRICH, PARTNER IN THE JEWELRY FIRM OF HYDE & Goodrich, the house that once stood at the corner of Orange and Annunciation Streets—and which now overlooks Coliseum Square—displays a simple dignity. A raised center hall cottage, it conforms to a plan that has been ubiquitous in the American South for centuries. Decorated in restrained Greek Revival style, it faces the street with a wide front porch supported by Doric pillars and crowned with a dentilated entablature. Flanked by pilasters, the large front door adds another stately detail. But dormers protruding from the pitched roof offer a less formal note to the cottage, which might as comfortably stand in a small Southern town as in the elegant enclave of New Orleans' Lower Garden District.

When the Creole developer, Armand Duplantier, purchased the plantation land upriver from the American District from Madame Delord-Sarpy, he named it Faubourg Annonciation. Although Delord-Sarpy had already retained the French surveyor and architect Barthelemy Lafon to devise a plan for subdividing her plantation, Duplantier expanded the commission. He asked Lafon to draw a new plan that was "by far the grandest urban scheme yet devised in New Orleans or, indeed, in the entire Mississippi Valley," according to historian Fred Starr.[1] The plan included a grand canal called the Cours des Tritons (after the forked scepter of Neptune); a circular park called Place du Tivoli, named after the town near Rome; and two large parks, one with a coliseum and the other with a cathedral to be called Place de l'Annonciation.

"Lafon's basins, fountains and tree-lined canals and streets, with market places, parks and monumental buildings, were conceived by him to create an environment of classic beauty and formality," write Mary Louise Christovich, Roulhac Toledano, and Betsy Swanson in their introduction to *New Orleans Architecture, Vol. 1: The Lower Garden District*.[2] A rather less elaborate reality evolved out of this grand vision. Neither the coliseum nor the cathedral was

[1] S. Frederick Starr, *Southern Comfort: The Garden District of New Orleans* (New York: Princeton Architectural Press, 1998), p. 193.

[2] Mary Louise Christovich, et al., *New Orleans Architecture, Vol. 1: The Lower Garden District* (Gretna, LA: Friends of the Cabildo and Pelican Publishing, 1971), p. xiii.

built and only one of the system of interweaving canals and
basins was dug. But three main parks were created, becoming today's Lee Circle, Annunciation Square, and Coliseum
Square. Instead of imposing a rigid grid, the planner let the
shape of the river influence his street plan, which included
small public green spaces that remain as pocket parks
throughout the neighborhood.

The plan provided lots large enough to accommodate spacious villas surrounded by front and side gardens, a
factor that gave rise to the neighborhood's late-twentieth-
century name, the Garden District. Another of Lafon's
enduring contributions is a romantically classical nomencla-
ture for the streets, including Clio, Terpsichore, and
Melpomene to honor the muses, as well as avenues named
for wood and river nymphs. In the 1850s, promoters
advertised the neighborhood north of St. Charles Avenue as
"Melpomenia," a term that has been revived today.

Lafon ultimately abandoned architecture, "and in
later years he drifted into other activities, including piracy
and the study of Egyptian hieroglyphics."[3] But elements of
his plan endured, inspiring flights of fancy and a diversity of
architectural styles Starr calls "bewildering."[4] The Anglo-

---

[3]Starr, p. 17.

[4]Ibid.

American businessmen who settled there built mansions, suburban villas, and country cottages that drew upon Georgian, vernacular Southern, Greek Revival, and even Orientalist sources. These contrasted with the structures of the French Quarter and the American Sector, where narrow, urban lots spawned more uniform building types and relatively homogeneous façades.

Despite the architectural variety of the neighborhood, the style to gain the greatest popularity was the Greek Revival. In 1979, a New Orleans' preservation organization called Friends of the Cabildo declared the Lower Garden District, "one of the most comprehensive nineteenth-century Greek Revival neighborhoods remaining in this country"— and also one of New Orleans most threatened areas. When a generation of young New Orleanians abandoned the city's urban neighborhoods for the suburbs after World War II, the Lower Garden District began to lose luster and fell victim to urban planning schemes. When the Mississippi River Bridge Authority constructed a ramp leading to the Greater New Orleans Bridge at the downtown end of Coliseum Square, the neighborhood sank deeper into disrepair.

ABOVE: While restoring the house, the owners discovered the brass tracks of pocket doors that had been replaced in the mid-nineteenth century by interior columns. The Griffins and their architect re-created the pocket doors, surrounding them with Doric pilasters that echo the house's façade decoration.

Fortunately, preservationists and urban pioneers came to the rescue in the 1970s. The Friends of the Cabildo launched their study of the neighborhood, which became the first in the New Orleans Architecture series, and urban pioneers, including Camille and Duncan Strachan, began buying and restoring threatened properties. Mr. Strachan, who grew up in the Garden District, and Mrs. Strachan, later a trustee of the National Trust for Historic Preservation, bought a house overlooking Coliseum Square where they raised their family. Joined by friends Thomas and Kathryn Favrot, they subsequently rescued the Goodrich-Stanley House from demolition by neglect in 1981. Purchasing it for $101 from the New Orleans Parish School Board, they moved the cottage from Annunciation Square to its new site on Coliseum Square—a lot slated for the construction of a condominium project that threatened the area's architectural integrity.

While the Strachans and Favrots supervised and funded the move, reconstruction, and exterior restoration of the Goodrich-Stanley House with the help of architects Henry

Krotzer and Sam Wilson of Koch and Wilson, they hoped to find a buyer to complete the interior work. "We were so lucky the Griffins came along," Mrs. Strachan exclaims. Dr. Jeffrey and Barbara Griffin felt equally fortunate to find the spacious cottage for sale. Mrs. Griffin, who had previously lived in the neighborhood, and her husband both dreamed of living on Coliseum Square and were searching for a raised cottage that would accommodate their growing family.

Although the house's façade looked pristine, the interior was a disaster with filthy carpeting, acoustical tile ceilings, and missing plaster, doors, and mantels. Yet the original cypress flooring, door and window surrounds, and staircase remained. Taking clues from the extant details, the Griffins and architect Peter Trapolin renovated the interior, making new doors by copying ones found in the house and recreating pocket doors that originally divided the double parlors. These had been replaced with interior columns, probably in the 1850s by the house's second owner, an English cotton merchant named Henry Hope Stanley, who imposed a more formal décor upon the house.

BELOW: The Griffins enclosed the back porch of the house to improve the flow of traffic from the main house to the attached service wing. Rustic antiques from Louisiana plantations decorate the porch.

With Mr. Trapolin's help, the Griffins returned the cottage to its original simple elegance, thickening some walls to incorporate bathrooms and closets while maintaining the overall flow of rooms. In the old kitchen wing, they created a modern kitchen and an informal dining area that overlooks a patio garden. Although the Griffins' collection of European and Louisiana antiques is traditional, it is mixed with contemporary furniture and art that give the large, airy rooms a timeless elegance.

Should the house's most famous resident, the eccentric explorer Lord Henry Morton Stanley, who jumped ship as a cabin boy in the New Orleans harbor and lived for some time as the foster-child of Henry Stanley and his wife, defy time to return to his boyhood home—he might feel quite at ease. Certainly the bronze plaque in front of the house relating the highlights of his career, from his most famous utterance ("Dr. Livingston, I presume.") to his knighting by the King of Belgium, would have delighted him.

83

Eccentric

NEW ORLEANS

RENOWNED FOR PICTURESQUE DECREPITUDE, TROPICAL LANGUOR, AND LICENTIOUS sensuality, New Orleans defines decadence. It has spawned a stream of bohemians whose flamboyant outpourings of music, dance, and word have entranced the world. With its blend of French, Spanish, Caribbean, African, English, American, German, and Italian citizens, the city stakes claim as America's most exotic destination. When defined as "outside the ordinary," the term eccentric clearly describes the unique culture, architecture, and lifestyle that evolved out of this seething milieu.

New Orleans' collective eccentricity finds passionate expression each year during Carnival, which begins on Twelfth Night and ends with Mardi Gras. "[T]he colonial orphan's longing for the crown, the perpetual calendar of fantasy (of preparations, enactment, and of memory), the passions for music and dance—all have been played out amid New Orleans' extravagant vegetation, beneath her blazing suns and warlock moons."[1] These are the words with which Henri Schindler, the festival's most dedicated historian, describes the city's annual lapse into enchanted ritual.

Spangled floats seem perpetually to travel New Orleans' streets, bedecked with blossoms, birds, and effigies of mythological, historic, and political beings. Not limited to Carnival, parades also honor saints favored by the city's population, including St. Patrick (who earns three separate parades) and St. Joseph (who is also celebrated in Italian homes and churches with fanciful altars stacked high with food). Gaudy beads, heavy cabbages, and miscellaneous trinkets are tossed to crowds who don costumes, gild nearly naked bodies, or sit on porches imbibing intoxicants throughout the day and night.

Within such a setting, it is not surprising that people create eccentric domestic environments: rooms decorated with altarlike arrangements of peculiar *objets*, spaces pervaded with sensual excess or melancholic drama, or decorative schemes that play clever variations upon the city's myriad themes. *Vive la différence* is the motto of these New Orleanians who tap deeply into their city's worldly and other-worldly culture.

PAGE 84: Floats under construction in the Rex krewe's den depict the theme, "The Winged World," conceptualized to illustrate myths involving birds.

OPPOSITE: Ecclesiastical paintings and sculptures mix with whimsical pieces including a mirror designed by Mario Villa in the designer's Garden District pied-à-terre.

---

[1]Henri Schindler, *Mardi Gras, New Orleans* (Paris–New York: Flammarion, 1997), p. 8.

86

Luxurious History

The Home of Ersy Schwartz

AN ESPLANADE RIDGE MANSION

"AS MYSTERIOUS AND LOVELY AS A VEILED WOMAN, GLIMPSED BRIEFLY IN A PASSING CROWD, is the old Fisk home on Esplanade," wrote Edith Elliot Long in a 1966 article in the *Vieux Carré Courier* describing the house now inhabited by artist Ersy Schwartz and photographer Kyle Roberts. "Set in the rear of its lot, half-hidden by vestiges of a parterred garden, sheltered behind a high brick wall, the house can be seen only through openings in one of the most celebrated gates in the city. It seems to dwell in a kind of purdah, suspended forever in time and space, its strange beauty tinged with immortality."

Decades later, the house on Esplanade Avenue is still suggestive of mystery and the veiled withdrawal of purdah. Its severe brick façade, punctuated by tall, shuttered openings, is just visible through the dark scrollwork of the gate. A black fountain presides over the lawn, its jets still and its basin filled with water that reflects the sky in inky darkness. Removed from the bustling energy of the avenue where cars rush and dogs romp in the neutral ground (local parlance for the median of a divided boulevard), the house seems encased in breathless silence, like the taxidermied birds and flowers Victorian ladies arranged beneath glass domes as table decorations.

Just such an object, its Victoriana infused with sly surrealism, stands in the immense formal parlor that stretches behind the façade's French doors. Beneath the tall glass dome, Ms. Schwartz' dead pet parakeet finds eternal rest. "I stuffed [Sam] and gave him a step ladder to ascend on," the artist explains. This objét d'art shares a tabletop with another of Ms. Schwartz's assemblages, a winged mask of bronze made in 1984 decorated with pheasant feathers and iron pen quill tips. "I am obsessed with detail, perfection of form, and the making of objects," says Ms. Schwartz, whose sculptures and assemblages reveal the artist's fascination with the craftsmanship of centuries past.

An artist who taught at New York's Cooper Union School of Art and exhibits internationally, Ms. Schwartz returned to New Orleans to care for her mother several years ago. She moved back into the Esplanade Avenue house that has been in her family for three

OPPOSITE: **Although the interior features extensive Greek Revival–style moldings, particularly in the large drawing room, the exterior of the house is minimally decorated. A cast-iron gallery surmounted by a wrought-iron balcony does little to offset the severity of the brick façade.**

89

ABOVE: Sculptural
assemblages by Ersy
Schwartz infuse the formal
parlor with surrealism.

OPPOSITE: This elegant
stairway dates from the
early twentieth century.
Before it was installed,
the upstairs bedrooms were
accessed from the exterior.

generations and where she spent her teenage years after growing up in the Pontalba Apartments on Jackson Square. "It was a real neighborhood then," she recalls of her first home in the French Quarter's heart. "The French Market really functioned as it should have with a butcher, a fish monger, fresh vegetables, a poultry purveyor, many accoutrements that have since vanished . . . Reuters Seeds, Desporte Pharmacy, mapmakers, working wharves."

When Ms. Schwartz moved back into the house on Esplanade Avenue as an adult, she discovered "a private place which serves as a wonderful retreat." Filled with family heirlooms including massive mahogany bedroom furnishings from New Orleans' renowned Mallard workshop and a Rococo Revival parlor set, the house suits Ms. Schwartz and Ms. Roberts perfectly. "We share the same tastes for old things and for drowning in luxurious history," says Ms. Schwartz.

Inspired by her childhood experiences in New Orleans, whether the masking and pageantry of Carnival, the decayed opulence of old houses with exquisitely crafted details, the South's general air of Gothic romanticism, or the city's specific faith in saints, specters, and spectacles, Ms. Schwartz creates work that reflects her surroundings and "looks like it was made for this eccentric space." These include a parasol made of gloves hung with a veil of satin ribbons that was part of Ms. Schwartz's costume for the St. Ann parade. Made from the gloves of the deceased mother of one of the parade's players, the fluttering parasol hovers like a ghost among the parlor's highly wrought decorations.

"Ceilings float high above the head, richly decked in cornices and moldings. Great doorways are magnificently trimmed. Plaster rosettes adorn the centers of the ceilings. This is Greek Revival at its best," enthuses the author of the aforementioned article. These late nineteenth-century details remain today, their ornate majesty reflected in the shadowy silver-backed mirror that hangs above a marble mantel. Six hundred volumes of French and English literature now line the room—a legacy of the Schwartz family, who are the third family to inhabit the house.

Ornamented in the Greek
Revival style, the parlor
features an American,
late-nineteenth-century
Rococo Revival suite of
rosewood furniture and a
selection of Ms. Schwartz's
artworks, including
a ghostly parasol made
of gloves.

93

Like a shell, the house reveals the gradual accretions of its residents, beginning with the Fisk family, who purchased two adjoining lots on Esplanade Avenue before the Civil War. During the war, when they sought sanctuary in Flat Rock, North Carolina, the family gained several new members through weddings and births and lost others to battle and illness. The reconfigured family returned to New Orleans where the widow Fisk moved into a simple, one-story house set back from the street next door to her son Edward's more stately home. Mrs. Fisk sold the house in 1871 to Aristide Hopkins, during whose residence a second story was added along with a wooden gallery. Slender cast-iron columns support the gallery, which is ornamented on the second floor with a wrought-iron railing.

When the house was sold in 1925 to Myrthe Stauffer Schwartz, the current resident's grandmother, yet more changes and additions were made. Under the guidance of well-known New Orleans architect Richard Koch, the house was remodeled to include an interior staircase, the rear façade of the dining room was redesigned and additional interior decoration was added, including four marble mantels brought by Mrs. Schwartz from her family home, which was demolished and replaced by the Orpheum Theatre.

When the current resident's family moved into the house in 1964, her mother left the architecture unchanged, perpetuating a gracious, social lifestyle shared by generations. "My parents were full of life," Ms. Schwartz reminisces. "Most of their friends were artists and writers. This house has hosted many a fine lot of times: elaborate dinner parties and get-togethers, weddings and funerals." Ms. Schwartz and Ms. Roberts continue these traditions as preservationists not only of this family home, but of a way of life that is threatened as so many neighboring houses are turned into time-shares and condominiums. "I intend to keep this house in my family for as long as there is someone here who loves it and cares about keeping it a single dwelling as much as I do," Ms. Schwartz declares.

LEFT: A black velvet cap with cast bronze wings made by Ms. Schwartz sits on the foot of this bed and taxidermied emu legs stand on the mantel.

RIGHT: Ms. Schwartz made every piece of this sculptural bed by hand, from the bronze hardware to the mahogany framework.

Amormysterii

The Home of Henri Schindler

A FRENCH QUARTER CREOLE TOWNHOUSE

"HORRORVACUI" IS AN ART HISTORICAL TERM COBBLED TOGETHER FROM TWO LATIN words meaning fear of empty space. It is used to describe the work of artists who obsessively cover every inch of their canvas or paper with marks. The term springs to mind when visiting the home of Henri Schindler, one of New Orleans' foremost experts on Mardi Gras traditions and an avid collector of Carnival ephemera. But deeper inspection reveals another impulse at play upon the crowded walls and surfaces of his bijou apartment in an early nineteenth-century Creole townhouse. *Amormysterii* better describes the passion that fuels the life and fills the living quarters of this devotee of mysteries, both sacred and profane.

Mr. Schindler saw his first Carnival celebration in 1946 at the age of five, when the annual festival beginning on Twelfth Night and ending on Mardi Gras returned to the streets and ballrooms of New Orleans after a wartime hiatus. "I was totally fascinated and smitten, and became somewhat preoccupied with it," he recalls. Young Henri was entranced not only by the gaudy fancy of the floats and costumes, but also by the air of secrecy that surrounded their creation and the antique rituals that inspired the practice.

When his father considered moving to another state, Mr. Schindler (then nine or ten) begged a man he had met who was involved in making floats to allow him in the den, as the secret construction sites are known, so that he could get one last glimpse of the magical creations. "That was the beginning of my coming into the inside," says the man whose early initiation led to a life devoted to the research of Mardi Gras' secrets and the perpetuation of its most profound practices.

"Many people just think, 'Cheesy, tacky, booze, boobs,' when they think about Mardi Gras—but there's more to it than that," says Mr. Schindler, the author of three books on the festival that was first celebrated in New Orleans with formal dances in 1743. The roots of Carnival date back far earlier to religious rites practiced in ancient Greece and Rome and perpetuated in Italy and France through the Middle Ages until the present day. "There is an

OPPOSITE: The Greek Revival cypress mantel is decorated as an altar to Proteus, the Greek god of transformation who inspired the eponymous Carnival krewe. Painted fans adorned with faux-plumes and stylized lotus blossoms are French stage props that may have been used in a production of *Aida*.

97

aspect of New Orleans' Carnival that has been sorely neglected—a very rich and wonderful artistic legacy, which is one of the reasons people are so imprinted with it and have been for almost 200 years," he explains.

"Human bodies are seen with heads of beasts and birds, beasts and birds with human heads; demi-beasts, demi-fishes, snakes' heads and bodies with arms of apes; manbats from the moon; mermaids; satyrs, beggars, monks, and robbers parade and march on foot, on horseback, in wagons, carts, coaches," wrote New Orleans Mayor James Creecy, describing the Mardi Gras of 1835.[1] Only words remain to recall these early parades, but by the second half of the nineteenth century, images began to survive to demonstrate the artistry of Carnival. The oldest known one is a sketch for a 1858 Mistick Krewe of Comus float entitled "Flora Drawn by Butterflies," which depicts the dainty goddess and her winged team atop a fire truck decorated with garlands and plumes.[2]

Mr. Schindler began amassing his private collection of Carnival ephemera in the early 1960s when he moved from Algiers Point to the French Quarter. He began frequenting antique shops where he discovered old ball invitations like those he had only seen before in museums. "It had never occurred to me that these things could be purchased," he recalls, describing how the antique stores reminded him of Aladdin's cave. One of these antiques dealers, Juanita Elfert, introduced Mr. Schindler to his mentor, Louis Fischer, the *grande-dame* of Mardi Gras conceptualization and design from the 1920s through the '70s.

Through Fischer, Mr. Schindler found his calling as an artistic director who delves into mythology, natural history, the annals of Mardi Gras, and the world of

[1] Quoted in Henri Schindler, *Mardi Gras* (New Orleans, Paris–New York: Flammarion, 1997), p. 22.

[2] Schindler, pp. 36, 42.

Late nineteenth-century Aesthetic Movement furniture decorates the living room, its shell-like forms complementing a collection of sea shells that honors the Greek sea god Proteus. A screens covered with *decoupage* made from scraps of late nineteenth-century color lithography stands in a corner.

A plaster bust of Pope
Benedict XV peers from
one corner of the room
Mr. Schindler calls
The Holy Office. An
exquisitely embroidered
silk robe, believed to
date from seventeenth-
or eighteenth-century
Europe, belonged to a
previous resident who
descended from an
Austrian family.

contemporary politics and social culture to find themes that inspire whole parades, individual floats, and ball decorations. Mr. Schindler has offered this service for several of New Orleans' most august krewes, as Carnival's organizations are called, including Comus, Momus, and Rex, working with teams of artists and craftspeople to supervise the translation of these themes into fleeting reality.

Relics of his passion fill Mr. Schindler's apartment—ball invitations, glass beads, a tiny mask used as a party favor, a pair of white boots worn by a Carnival captain. The mantel of the living room is decorated as an altar to Proteus—the sea god who changed appearance at will, thus inspiring the eponymous Creole krewe that parades in costume on the eve of Mardi Gras. Seashell encrusted goblets and pearls adorn the mantel, as well as a pair of gilded sacred hearts that symbolize the French roots of the krewe formed in the nineteenth century.

To one side of the mantel stands a bejeweled satin hat that Mr. Schindler calls his "triple tiara." He wore the towering headpiece several times while portraying popes and papal themes in Carnival parades. One year, he dressed the part of Pius IX, personifying the doctrine of Papal Infallibility in a parade concerned with Delusions of Grandeur. Another year, he wore the hat along with chains in the role of the Babylonian Captivity of the Church for a Babylonian-themed spectacle. He wore it again as Pope Leo X in a parade devoted to sybaritic legends.

ABOVE RIGHT: A papier-maché bust of Pius XII sits on the mantel of the Holy Office against the backdrop of a French or Flemish religious banner.

RIGHT: A frame fitted with a pair of white silk boots worn by the captain of an early-twentieth-century Mardi Gras parade.

Papal portraits and appurtenances make up the second largest portion of Mr. Schindler's collection of cherished objets. Scattered throughout the house, they form the central theme of a room Mr. Schindler calls The Holy Office. In this small room with deep gold walls there are five busts of popes including a plaster effigy of Benedict XV gazing with otherworldly calm out of a shadowy corner and a papier-mâché portrait of Pius XII that Mr. Schindler commissioned because "that was how it all began."

The collector is referring to his second lifelong preoccupation: a fascination with the rituals of the Roman Catholic Church. This interest took wing with the death of Pius XII in 1958, when the teenage Mr. Schindler first observed the pomp and rituals surrounding papal funerals and elections. Born in a Catholic hospital called Hôtel Dieu staffed by nuns in starched white hats resembling seagull wings, Mr. Schindler may have been predisposed to this obsession, which eventually took him to Rome to witness firsthand the election of John Paul I in 1978. There, the New Orleanian attended the Mass of the Holy Spirit and watched for puffs of smoke from the Vatican signaling the election's status.

In Mr. Schindler's dining room, mementos of the sacred and the profane mingle in congenial proximity. While one sideboard holds a collection of tin toys from the 1920s and '30s, another displays a disparate assembly including a crystal bust of Pius IX draped with a silver mask, a dance card from a Carnival ball decorated with a wax hand, old beads, and paste tiaras. While such a mingling might seem eccentric or irreverent outside New Orleans (except, perhaps, in Venice), it passes for near normal in a city where pageants, both on the street and in the cathedral, are practiced with habitual fervor.

"[M]asquerades are very frequent," wrote a shocked English reformer visiting the city in the mid-nineteenth century. "Even religion itself is made a matter of show and spectacle. . . . A high-mass is regarded as a great attraction, and Easter Sunday as something like the benefit night of a popular actor." Mr. Schindler, who does not discriminate between sacred and secular mysteries, expresses delight, not dismay, at his city's celebratory tendencies. "We are very fortunate to live in a place that is so rooted in the fantastic," he exclaims.

OPPOSITE: The top of a sideboard in the dining room is scattered with bibelots, including a small crystal bust of Pius IX adorned with a tiny silver mask.

LEFT: Gargantuan images of a dissected tortoise and a dismembered mosquito—educational lithographs from the early twentieth-century—offer disquieting kitchen décor. "I would gladly have bought more if I thought I could find room for them," says Mr. Schindler, who left a lobster and three other animals behind at the antiques shop.

103

Villa's Villa

The Studio and Pied-à-Terre of Mario Villa

A GARDEN DISTRICT ITALIANATE VILLA

"SILENCE ALLOWS US TO RETREAT TO THAT PLACE WHERE WE CAN FIND OUT WHO WE ARE," writes internationally acclaimed artist, sculptor, furniture designer, and collector Mario Villa. He invites those who encounter his work to discover within themselves "that quiet place where we can retreat and simply define that which surrounds us and the reason and use for it." Exuberant and extraverted, the personality of the multi-talented artist seems upon first encounter to be at odds with this thoughtful entreaty to solitude. But every extravert conceals an introvert, and so does Mr. Villa.

Although his work is collected by a globe-trotting group of glitterati including Karl Lagerfeld and Princess Caroline of Monaco, Mr. Villa chooses to live and work in the languid atmosphere of New Orleans. He found his way there when his family sought refuge in America after the Sandinista revolution exiled them from their native Nicaragua in 1979. A self-described sensualist and iconoclast, Mr. Villa felt at home in the city where he earned degrees in anthropology and architecture at the University of New Orleans and Tulane University, respectively.

"I was forced to create my own little world," Mr. Villa explained to an interviewer in 1991.[1] "When your identity has been shaken, you look into yourself and say, what do I like?" He responded to this question by making and surrounding himself with art and objéts that recalled (and include a portion of) the collection his family built and cherished over several generations. His great-grandfather was a doctor during the Mexican Revolution who "ran into the burning churches and literally rescued the artworks that he regarded as part of the national patrimony."[2] These and other pieces of ecclesiastical art form the heart of the artist's collection, which includes polychrome-wood depictions of saints, gilt-framed portraits of royalty and religious figures, antique French and Italian furniture, and pre-Columbian pottery.

OPPOSITE: The pink stucco villa designed by Myrlin McCullar in the 1940s shares many of the hallmarks of earlier Garden District Italianate homes, including the exaggerated cornices, bold window surrounds, and severe geometry.

[1]Mimi Read, "Bayou Baroque," *House & Garden*, June 1991, n.p.

[2]Ibid.

Objects designed by Mr. Villa, including the welded steel table with brass and bronze details, three small paintings of faces, and glass sculptures, share space with antiques and contemporary paintings.

ABOVE: Eighteenth-century heads of saints and a seventeenth-century portrait miniature of a Florentine cardinal are among cherished artworks standing atop a console in the living room.

Soon after completing his education, Mr. Villa turned to furniture design to make a living, creating sculptural metal pieces that embodied his fascination with classical forms and antique art. Marrying the attenuated lines and whimsical decoration of the architecture depicted in Pompeii's paintings with the plastic vigor of Giacometti, the artist's designs also demonstrate a passion for craftsmanship. Whether a table with legs in the form of bronze figures bound with coils of brass or a bed with spike-y posts and a headboard of gilded *verre églomisé*, Mr. Villa's work reveals an obsession with hand-worked matter.

Not surprisingly, this artist's hands rarely rest. He continually invents new bodies of work including fluidly rendered drawings of faces, towering glass sculptures combining mask-like faces with decorative motifs, or bronze lamps shaped like abstract figures. Perhaps this restless creativity explains why Mr. Villa did not stop after designing one extraordinary home for himself in New Orleans—a carmine sanctuary behind the modest Greek Revival façade of a shot-gun house in sleepy Faubourg St. John. The artist has lived there for nearly fifteen years, surrounded by Venetian red walls hung salon style with European paintings and adorned with crystal chandeliers, tapestries, and his own neo-Roman furniture.

This house is a luxurious, maximalist lair, which may be another reason Mr. Villa decided to create a second, more minimalist abode. Located in the Garden District, this pied-à-terre and office fills the penthouse of an Italianate villa built in the 1940s by Myrlin McCullar, one of New Orlean's best mid-century architects. Reputedly inspired by a villa in Venice, the tall, pink, stuccoed house features exaggerated cornices, boldly ornamented fenestration including round windows wreathed with garlands, and a pair of rampant griffons in plaster relief.

It is not surprising that such a fanciful palazzo should attract Mr. Villa. Elaine Uddo, who bought the house in the 1970s and who rents the penthouse apartment to Mr. Villa, described it as Mr. McCullar's showcase. "He put everything into this house that any client could possibly desire for a home," she notes, including beautiful moldings and a three-story staircase with hand-wrought metal banisters and railings. "The quality of the work is first class," Mr. Villa agrees. "The craftsmanship of the 1940s is something we have lost."

Unlike Mr. Villa's Faubourg St. John house, where light filters in through louvered shutters, a shaded gallery, and surrounding plants, his penthouse is radiant with bright, unfettered sunshine. The creamy walls reflect the light, allowing the silhouettes of sculptural furnishings—whether the artist's own designs or curvaceous French antiques—to show off their calligraphic forms. In such an airy setting, the religious art and artifacts seem to shed some of their weight and somberness. And Mr. Villa's designs, whether large pieces of furniture or decorative lamps and objects, have more room to breathe and express their playful elegance in the large, bright rooms.

Mr. Villa is a designer who has contributed much to the evolving look of new New Orleans. His Garden District domain demonstrates his newest interpretation of New Orleans style—one that moves out of dark-hued decadence into an elegant minimalism that still celebrates the city's European roots. In both his houses, this Latin-born cosmopolitan mingles elements from his own background with those from New Orleans' collective past to create a sanctuary that is at once personal and global. "Those are pre-Columbian ceramics, these are Venetian paintings, that is a French bed . . . that is what I love about New Orleans. We dare to mix."

LEFT: An eighteenth-century Villa family portrait hangs above a writing table where several more faces painted by Mr. Villa sit. Mr. Villa also designed the welded steel and *verre églomisé* bed, the bench at its foot, and the glass sculpture and lamp that sit beside it.

Neo-Neoclassical

The Home of Trish and Lewis Stirling

AN UPTOWN COURTYARD DWELLING

OPPOSITE: A two-tone paving treatment with areas of gray gravel creates a contemporary, geometric floor for the front porch. The Philippe Starck chairs of white resin provide perches for viewing the Mardi Gras parades that file down St. Charles Avenue.

"ST. CHARLES AVENUE BECAME THE LOCATION OF CHOICE FOR THE WEALTHIER ANGLO-Americans," writes architectural historian Roulhac Toledano about turn-of-the-nineteenth-century development along the central artery of uptown New Orleans. "[T]heir parade of eclectic building styles . . . follows the bend in the river to present a lavish display of monumental and gaudy two-story houses."[1] Not long ago, Trish and Lewis Stirling lived in just such a house, a Beaux Arts style mansion furnished with an eclectic collection of American and European antiques and contemporary furniture and art.

The twentieth century witnessed the rapid rise, decline, and reascendance of real estate values along the wide boulevard bisected by the St. Charles Avenue streetcar line. During the mid-century period, many residents sold their homes, relocating to modern suburbs. A significant number of the more exotic and lavish mansions were torn down, replaced with architecturally undistinguished apartment buildings, retail establishments, and single family homes that created intrusions of inappropriate style and scale. By 1975, a portion of the avenue was named a local historic district and homeowners once more began to recognize the aesthetic value of the beleaguered neighborhood. The Stirlings were among the pioneers who began purchasing and refurbishing properties in the area.

In 2000, when their son left for college, the couple sold the large house they had lived in for six years and began the hunt for a new home. After viewing many properties, they despaired of finding the perfect one until they visited a house Ms. Stirling describes as "a blank canvas on St. Charles Avenue." She and her husband Lewis, who has a degree in construction management, quickly recognized the swan that lay hidden within the plain duckling. "We drove to a nearby restaurant and began sketching. We drew a plan for the façade and realized that it would work," Trish recalls.

[1] Roulhac Toledano, *The National Trust Guide to New Orleans* (New York: John Wiley & Sons, Inc., 1966), p. 157.

The couple put in an offer and soon began renovating the 1964 brick house that looked more like a fortress than a home with its small windows, high fence, and brick and metal columns. The Stirlings reenvisioned the façade as a contemporary neoclassical design, with a row of Doric pillars crowned with a parapet similar to those employed on area houses. "We knew we needed the height of the parapet to make the scale more appropriate," explains Ms. Stirling. But they kept the design of the parapet simple, eschewing dentils and other details.

Eleven-foot ceilings were one of the house's main attractions, but small windows and low doors countered this generous height. So the Stirlings opened them upwards, creating exterior openings more in keeping with a nineteenth-century sense of scale. They also raised the interior doors to the height of eight feet, tore out walls dividing the interior space into small rooms, and replaced sliding-glass doors surrounding the interior courtyard with tall French doors. "I think the original occupants were concerned about security, yet they wanted to bring the outside indoors," says Ms. Stirling, explaining the focus of the house upon its interior courtyard.

The atrium, a common architectural feature of the sixties and seventies, oddly enough provides one of several traditional New Orleans elements to the renovated home. Like the eighteenth- and nineteenth-century structures built downriver by Creoles, the house's interior addresses its courtyard as much or more than the street, drawing light, air, and a sense of calm from the enclosed space. The French doors opening onto the courtyard, albeit glazed with UV-glass, create another traditional reference, just as the neo-neoclassical Greek Revival porch marries classical and contemporary styles.

While at first glance, the interior is unmistakably modern—an early twenty-first-century reinterpretation of sixties *mod* style—closer inspection reveals an eclectic approach to decorating with family possessions in keeping with traditional New Orleans interiors. The bright paprika red velvet chairs, c. 1930s, that perch on a sea of deep white shag belonged to Ms. Stirling's grandmother. The nineteenth-century English grand piano that divides the dining area from the lounge came from Mr. Stirling's family. A lamp dating

from the 1950s came from Ms. Stirling's other grandmother, while simple gold-rimmed china and classic crystal glasses from her mother dress the dining room table.

"Family history is huge here," says Brian Bockman, the Stirlings' interior designer and a professor of architecture at Tulane University. "Instead of discarding old things that were out of style, they put them away, then brought them back out again. Here we are taking pieces that were dated ['but are coming back into fashion,' Trish interjects] and are updating them to a new time period." For example, a pair of chairs from the seventies were rechromed and

ABOVE: Walls were removed to create a flowing space that interior designer Brian Bockman divided into zones using white shag area rugs and dramatic features.

113

upholstered in pale blue bouclé to create stylish seating near to the kitchen. A whimsically shaped chair from the same period, once upholstered and skirted with flocked gold velvet, takes on new life clad in acid green dupioni and detailed with Tiffany-box blue buttons and cording.

Mr. Bockman calls these reinvented furnishings "new-told antiques." But the most striking reinvention of all is the chandelier hanging above the dining table—a crystal chandelier covered with a gleaming coat of bright candy apple red car paint. "I'd had the idea for a while, but I couldn't find anyone willing to risk painting a chandelier," says the designer, who has made his name in New Orleans designing strikingly contemporary hotel and restaurant interiors. "There's a decadence to taking a very expensive chandelier and painting it with high gloss car paint," he adds. "We named it Candy."

These are just the kinds of risks that Ms. Stirling wanted her designer to take. "I wanted the house to look like a hotel lobby," she claims—a statement that reveals a reaction to living for years in a formal, largely traditional home. The new house, with its spare architectural setting and lush, yet monochromatic textiles, provides an ideal backdrop for the Stirlings' collection of contemporary paintings, sculpture, and glass by local artists, as well as for colorful flower arrangements by the Stirlings' favorite florist, Stephen Sonnier of Dunn & Sonnier.

Ms. Stirling established a distinct design direction for the interior before engaging Mr. Bockman. She hung floor-length curtains of white silk dupioni that he describes as "very ball gown, very debutante" throughout the house. Then Mr. Bockman joined the team, bringing his own sense of history and daring to the project. "What I love about design in New Orleans is the city's eclectic nature and the people's personalities. People are willing to take risks because it's a decadent, fun city," he explains. "But they also bring their history with them."

OPPOSITE: **A red chandelier creates a lava-like explosion of color against a cool blue painting by Tina Stanley. French art deco chairs surround a table abloom with flowers from New Orleans florist Dunn & Sonnier.**

RIGHT: **A mahogany and gold sculpture by contemporary Cuban artist Jorge Gonzalez stands atop Louis Stirling's rare 86-key English piano.**

Row House Redux

Julia Row

THIRTEEN ROW TOWNHOUSES IN THE AMERICAN SECTOR

OPPOSITE: The design
of the thirteen row
townhouses comprising
Julia Row more closely
resembles that of early
nineteenth-century town-
houses in Baltimore or
Philadelphia than neigh-
boring Creole townhouses
in the French Quarter.

"JULIA ROW WAS ONCE THE BEST ADDRESS IN THE CITY AND LATER, ONE OF THE WORST—UNTIL 1976 when the Preservation Resource Center [PRC] restored and moved its headquarters into number 604."[1] This description of the thirteen row houses on Julia Street—nicknamed Millionaires' Row in the mid-nineteenth century and used as boarding houses with rooms and beds for rent in the early twentieth century—summarizes the mercurial history of the American Sector of New Orleans, from its development, through its turn-of-the-nineteenth-century decline, to its contemporary renaissance.

The block of brick townhouses between Camp Street and St. Charles Avenue was constructed in 1832 by the New Orleans Building Company as residences for the city's booming Anglo-American population. "That was the Golden Age of New Orleans, when Americans were flocking to the area," says Patricia Gay, director of the PRC, who worked in one of the buildings from 1976 until 2000, and has lived there from 2000 until the present. Ms. Gay refers to the decades following the Louisiana Purchase, when American traders and manufacturers from the Mid-West and the East Coast created their own business and residential neighborhood directly upriver from the French Quarter—a neighborhood that came to be called the American Sector.

"As in colonial situations around the world, the Anglo-Saxon newcomers to New Orleans encountered coolness and hostility," writes historian Fred Starr.[2] The newcomers, how-ever, were as wary of their predecessors as the Creoles were of them. They were also equally stubborn in their cultural and architectural self-expression. While the Creoles clung to building traditions inherited from France's tropical colonies—traditions that were quite suitable to New Orleans' subtropical climate—the American settlers insisted on transplanting East Coast build-ing practices that were far less appropriate to their new locale.

[1] William R. Mitchell, Jr., *Classic New Orleans* (New Orleans and Savannah: Martin-St. Martin Publishing Company, 1993), p. 106.

[2] Fred Starr, *Southern Comfort: The Garden District of New Orleans* (New York: Princeton Architectural Press, 1998), p. 14.

The houses designed by the then-New York–based architect James Dakin in collaboration with New Orleans architect Alexander Wood followed the Georgian English plan featuring a side stair hall, and were ornamented in a transitional style combining Federal and Greek Revival elements. Architect Benjamin Latrobe, a great proponent of Creole design, reviled the design of such row townhouses, which revealed the nearly unmodified architectural influence of Philadelphia and Baltimore—East Coast cities having little in common with New Orleans. He referred to them as "detestable, lopsided London house[s]," and decried their "red staring brickwork, imbibing heat thro' the whole unshaded substance of the wall."[3]

Despite these criticisms, the townhouses were immensely popular with Anglo-Americans and provided reassuringly familiar accommodations to some of the city's wealthiest transplants. With elegantly detailed entrances flanked by fluted Ionic columns and crowned with fanlights, the townhouses boasted spacious, high-ceilinged rooms with black marble mantels and plaster ceiling medallions in the form of acanthus leaves. While northeastern townhouses typically incorporated kitchens on their ground floors and servants quarters beneath the roofs, the townhouses of Julia Row include one-room-deep service wings at the rear, facing narrow courtyards designed to improve circulation. Galleries along the service wing façades and rear walls of the townhouses represent another concession to New Orleans' climate, creating a bit of French Quarter–style ambience, as do the second-story iron balconies on the front of the houses, which are accessed through tall windows and provide cross-ventilation for the double parlors.

While the townhouses enjoyed popularity in the decades before the Civil War, they fell out of favor in the late nineteenth century as Anglo-Americans moved further uptown to the Garden District and beyond, where they could build commodious villas better suited to the climate. The American Sector became more business oriented and its former residences were transformed into shops, offices, and tenements or torn down and replaced with warehouses and service stations. By 1900, Julia Row had become a tenement, subdivided into a warren of small apartments, and by the Depression, most of the townhouses became boarding houses,

ABOVE: An original entrance with delicate neoclassical details including transom fanlights with floral torches, garlanded oval sidelights, and fluted Ionic columns.

OPPOSITE: George Schmidt's portrait of Patricia Gay's son and daughter hangs above the Greek Revival mantel in the bedroom.

[3]Benjamin H. B. Latrobe, *Impressions Respecting New Orleans*, edited by Samuel Wilson, Jr. (New York: Columbia University Press, 1951), pp. 42, 106.

OPPOSITE: A painting by George Schmidt of a ghostly Carnival masker reflects in the mirrored door of an armoire attributed to New Orleans' renowned nineteenth-century Mallard furniture workshop.

BELOW: Over time, this space has served as a bathroom, dressing room, sewing room, and nursery. The footed bathtub came from a Garden District house inhabited by the Gay family for many years.

their once-gracious rooms filled with beds rented by the night. Its nadir, like its zenith, paralleled the fortunes of the neighborhood it graced.

"You had to slip on slimy things and step over people to get to work," recalls artist George Schmidt, who has maintained a studio in Julia Row since 1976, the same year the block attracted what might be called its most important twentieth-century occupant—the PRC. In danger of demolition-through-decay, the buildings attracted the notice of the preservation organization that works to rescue threatened neighborhoods by attracting residents and businesses. When one of the row houses became available for sale, the organization, then only two years old and strapped for funds, decided to buy it. With a state grant matched by funds raised through a now-annual party called Julia Jump, PRC purchased 604 Julia Street and transformed it into its headquarters, with a commercial space in the street-front space and an apartment above. "We were the first mixed-use building in the business district in modern times," states Ms. Gay.

Now, many blocks of Julia Street and its neighboring thoroughfares are lined with refurbished nineteenth- and early twentieth-century residential and commercial properties converted for mixed uses including art galleries, antique stores, restaurants, and professional offices on ground floors and residences above. Julia Row represents the most diverse—and most vibrant—of these. Private homes of artists, writers, and musicians—including Mr. Schmidt and band-mate Jack Stuart, whose eighteen-piece orchestra named the New Leviathan Oriental Fox-Trot Orchestra practices in another of the Row's townhouses. Converted into a firehouse in the late nineteenth century and subsequently an automotive repair shop called Precision Auto, the rehearsal space is nicknamed Precision Hall.

Eclectic furnishings including a turn-of-the-nineteenth-century Recamier couch, an early nineteenth-century bamboo sheet music cabinet, and an Edo period painted screen create a romantic, bohemian mood in Cassandra Sharpe's and Rich Look's front parlor. Mr. Look enjoys playing and composing on the 1954 Bösendorfer parlor grand piano he inherited from his maternal grandmother.

ABOVE: George Schmidt has a gallery in the ground floor level of one of the row's townhouses, a studio in the service ell behind, and a courtyard that serves as an open-air workspace.

OPPOSITE: The tables and mismatched chairs of Louisiana Products, located at 618 Julia Row, offer neighbors a place to sit and exchange news over a cup of chicory-laced coffee or a hot meal of Louisiana-style home cooking.

In the middle of the block, Louisiana Products offers basic provisions, hot meals of home style New Orleans cuisine, and what one visiting Chicagoan called "the best cup of coffee in New Orleans." Mr. Schmidt jokingly refers to its owner and operators, Martha and Melanie Owen, as the concierges of Julia Row, and Ms. Gay declares, "I don't know what I would do without them being there to greet me in the morning and evening and to discuss what's going on in the neighborhood and around the world." Rich Look, a producer, songwriter, and Japanese translator who lives in one of the townhouses with his wife, real-estate broker Cassandra Sharpe, calls Louisiana Products "the nerve center" for Julia Row's community of residents and business owners, who also include architects and antiques dealers.

These occupants coexist in a tightly knit community that recalls New Orleans' bohemian heyday in the early twentieth century when writers and musicians thrived in its eccentricity-friendly milieu. Even in more staid days when Julia Row was home to "the leading social element of the American colony," the townhouses were frequented by writers, including the editors of the *Picayune*, and musicians, including a society songstress who "sang, with inimitable pathos and wild passion," a song called "The Maniac," according to the memoir of nineteenth-century socialite, Eliza Ripley.[4]

In her 1912 memoir, Mrs. Ripley recounts how "a Mme. Peuch took possession of the house on the St. Charles street corner, and horrors! opened a boarding house, whereupon the aristocratic element gradually fluttered away." How delighted she would be to know that the block she envisioned languishing forever in decrepitude would gradually regain luster and survive another century or more.

[4]Eliza Ripley, *Social Life in Old New Orleans* (New York and London: D. Appleton and Co., 1912), pp. 167–72.

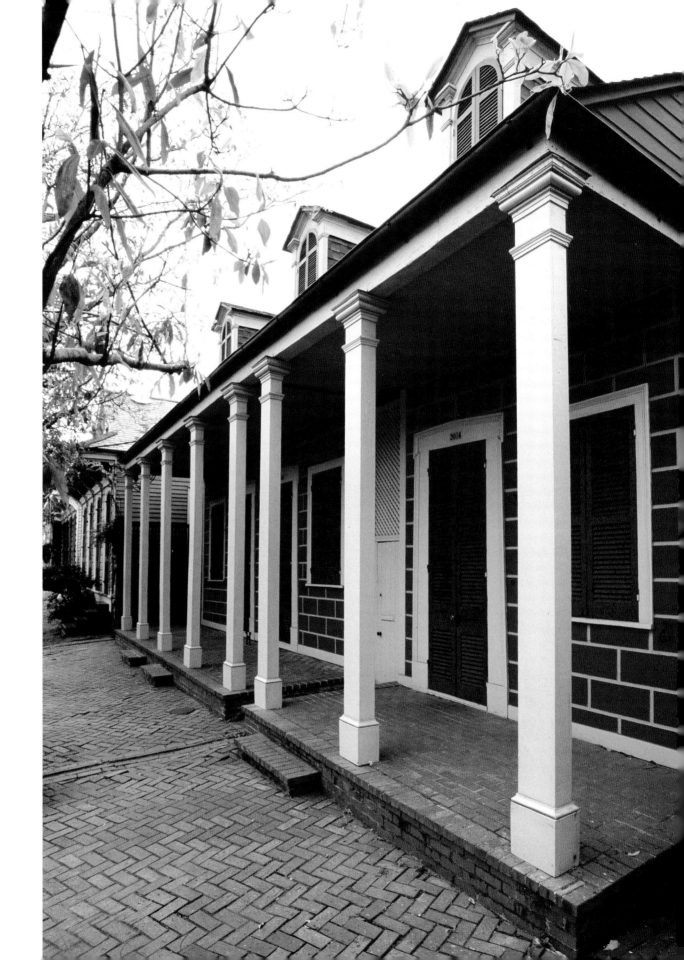

House Museum

The Home of Eugene Cizek and Lloyd Sensat

A FAUBOURG MARIGNY CREOLE COTTAGE

DR. EUGENE CIZEK, THE DIRECTOR OF PRESERVATION STUDIES AT TULANE UNIVERSITY, IS A scholar of environmental and social psychology as it relates to changing growth in city neighborhoods. Lloyd Sensat is an arts educator and co-founder with Cizek of the Education through Historic Preservation program that teaches children to study and value the buildings around them. They are the ideal interpreters for a Creole cottage on Burgundy Street whose past owners and inhabitants offer a remarkably thorough representation of ethnicities, professions, and social classes that comprised the population of nineteenth- and early twentieth-century New Orleans.

Not surprisingly, Dr. Cizek and Mr. Sensat see their house as much more than a home. Sun Oak Gardens, House Museum, and Guest House is their moniker for the property that once was part of the eighteenth-century sugar plantation Bernard Xavier Philippe de Marigny de Mandeville transformed into Faubourg Marigny in 1806. They live and work within its many rooms and extensive grounds, offer rooms to guests, and invite students and other visitors to tour the property. The pair also treats it as an ongoing archeological site still rich with untold history. Since Dr. Cizek and Mr. Sensat rescued it from neglect in the 1970s, they have conducted eighteen archeological excavations there, unearthing more than 40,000 artifacts now displayed alongside an extraordinary collection of Louisiana furniture.

Originally envisioned as a neighborhood for wealthy French and Creole residents, Faubourg Marigny was laid out with spacious lots, wide avenues including one named for Les Champs Elysées, and open squares inspired by Paris. The population of Faubourg Marigny, however, quickly diversified as its developer began subdividing large lots and selling them to middle class *gens des couleurs libre*, or free people of color. The objects unearthed at Sun Oak recount this history—the oldest being an intact eighteenth-century flask found in what may have been a cooling well for the plantation. Other artifacts date from the early nineteenth century, when Constance Rixner Bouligny, a free woman of color of French, German, and African descent, built a home on the property.

OPPOSITE: The rusticated façade of the nineteenth-century Creole cottage is composed of cypress boards scored to resemble stone. Three front doors open into three *infillade* suites of rooms.

127

ABOVE: A nineteenth-century carved walnut clock from Austria shares a wall with eighteenth-century hand-colored French prints of hot-air balloons and a Haitian folk art sunburst medallion.

OPPOSITE: A copy of a c. 1845 portrait of the house's mid-nineteenth-century residents, Asher Moses Nathan and his son Achille Lion, hangs in one of three front parlors. A c. 1800 walnut school-master's desk made in Paris stands beneath the portrait.

In keeping with popular architectural styles of that time, Bouligny constructed a brick-between-post Creole cottage in 1807, a simple one-and-a-half story structure using bricks as infill between vertical timbers, all covered with cypress weatherboards. Fifteen years later, Bouligny sold the cottage to Noël Carriere, a cooper and a free man of color, who in turn sold it in 1836 to Asher Moses Nathan, a Dutch-born Jew who rose to considerable success as a merchant in New Orleans.

It is to Nathan that the house owes much of its contemporary appearance. His fortunes high, Nathan remodeled the house, transforming it into a Greek Revival edifice with trabiated door surrounds and a porch with eight pillars. For an elegant finishing touch, Nathan had the cypress façade scored and painted to resemble glazed limestone. Today the façade is painted in a colorful palette derived from mid-nineteenth-century tradition with walls of French red and Creole putty and louvered doors and shutters painted bright Cuban blue.

Although his will indicates that he had a white, Catholic wife, Nathan lived in the house with a *placée*, or cohabitant, a free woman of color whose identity remains a mystery, and their two children, Achille and Anna. A copy of a portrait depicting Nathan holding hands with his son Achille Lion hangs in one of the house's parlors. The portrait was painted c. 1845 by Jules Lion, an artist of African and French descent who studied art in France, exhibited in the Paris Salons in the early 1830s, and introduced the daguerreotype to New Orleans. Lion was the godfather to the two children; his sister may have been Nathan's *placée*.

The house had several other residents including the American-born Algernon Sydney Lewis, son of native Virginian Judge James Lewis who was sent to New Orleans by Thomas Jefferson to establish American Law after the

Louisiana Purchase. Lewis bought the house in 1846 from Nathan, settling in the Creole quarter to satisfy his French wife, Annette Tronchet. Their son, Dr. Ernest Sidney Lewis, who grew up in the house, went on to become a chief surgeon in the Confederate army during the Civil War. Algernon's brother became mayor of New Orleans and founder of the prestigious Boston Club. The entire Lewis family is buried in aboveground tombs in the Historic St. Louis Cemetery Number One.

As the final decades of the nineteenth century unfolded and New Orleans fortunes waxed and waned, this great house—at one time including a total of thirty-six rooms, with twenty-seven in the main house and nine in a slave-quarter behind—was broken into three properties. With three front doors, each opening into rooms that flow in an *infillade* arrangement to terminate in individual staircases leading to second-floor rooms, the house was easily divided. By the late 1890s, the uptown side of the house was transformed into a laundry operated by a Chinaman and his wife, a white French Creole woman, who lived there with their six children. Dr. Cizek believes that the absence of interior plaster in this portion of the house is the result of the steamy atmosphere of the laundry. To this day, the bead-board paneling refuses to hold paint.

While the very walls of the house exude history lessons, the furnishings and decorations also tell the story of New Orleans and the surrounding Louisiana territory. A life-sized crucifix dominates a room in the downtown side of the house. Although it is an unsettling decoration for a dining room, the object is one of the finest in the owners' collection. "It is the original crucifix from the Spanish Saint Louis Cathedral that was built by Don Almonaster y Roxas in the late eighteenth century after the disastrous fire that destroyed much of the original French Quarter," explains Cizek. Carved from cypress, the crucifix was sold when the cathedral was torn down and replaced in the mid-nineteenth century. It ultimately made its way to a salvage and antiques shop where Dr. Cizek purchased it. Research by a historian colleague, William deMarigny Hyland, revealed the artifact's true provenance.

Paying testament to New Orleans' Spanish Catholic past, the crucifix sets the tone for a room that also includes a collection of figurines depicting saints ranging in style from the reverent to the kitsch. The chandelier illuminating the dining room once hung in the Quadroon Ballroom where well-heeled white men went to dance with free women of color in the first half of the nineteenth century. The light fixtures in the parallel suite of rooms came from a bordello in Storyville, the New Orleans neighborhood established in the late nineteenth century for legalized prostitution, which was also the birthplace of jazz. While they resemble the gasoliers prevalent in the 1880s and '90s, these lamps are examples of New Orleans' earliest electric fixtures.

OPPOSITE: The beaded lumber of this room, used for a period as a laundry, was originally painted. When the wood refused to hold another coat, the current residents carefully scraped it to reveal multi-colored vestiges of original paint. The wicker chaise longue was made in New Orleans and the 1840 Empire style armoire made of Louisiana walnut is a country piece from Opelousas.

ABOVE LEFT: A collection of figurines arranged on an antique jelly cabinet in the dining room pays homage to the many saints revered in New Orleans.

ABOVE RIGHT: A silver condiment holder, c. 1870, is a typical accoutrement of a nineteenth-century Creole dining room.

Cizek, whose maternal grandfather was a cabinetmaker in Prague, collects furniture and has filled the house with fine Louisiana armoires and *garde-mangers*, French chairs, and Mid-French antiques from the Cane and Red River Deltas of Central Louisiana. The severe lines and monumental bearing of the Louisiana-made furniture complement the simple elegance of the rooms that are sparely ornamented with Greek Revival mantels and doors surrounds. But notes of dark humor and decadent whimsy chime in at regular intervals to relieve the somber mood: the plaster and plastic saints in the dining room, a caned invalid's chair in the library, and a chaise longue of rattan with gold-tasseled velvet cushions that graces the former laundry. These details make the house a museum unlike any other where the past, in all its vibrant complexity, lives on to tell its story.

OPPOSITE: The dining room flows in an *infillade* arrangement into a small third room called a *cabinet* where a beautiful curving staircase leads to second floor bedrooms.

Elegant

NEW ORLEANS

A QUALITY OF REFINEMENT CHARACTERIZES NEW ORLEANS ARCHITECTURE, FROM ITS modest cottages to its stateliest mansions. There is the linearity of shotgun houses, their narrow rooms extending behind unpretentious façades, and the spare geometry of Creole cottages, with square faces, sloped roofs, and windows flanked by shutters. There is the calligraphy of iron balconies and galleries; the vertical severity of Italianate facades; and the gentler grace of Greek Revival porticoes that invite the visitor to step within.

This elegance speaks of a people who value beauty, domesticity, and hospitality. It also reveals the tenacity they required to construct—and preserve—such a city upon a crescent of swampy land. *A View of the Spanish Colony of the Mississippi*, published in Paris in 1803, describes the difficulties early inhabitants faced. "The peculiar humidity, which seems greater here than elsewhere, at certain times of the year reaches a point where everything spoils and moulds quickly; and it has even been noticed that the inside surface of the walls of houses newly constructed of bricks baked in New Orleans, is, at some times, so heavily saturated with moisture that water drips from it."

Yet it seems as if the challenges themselves—mercurial weather, miasma, and the absence of building materials other than soft local brick, tough cypress, and rough boards salvaged from Mississippi River flatboats—inspired the city's inhabitants to architectural transcendence. They honed their craft, incorporating the skills of immigrants from many lands, and imported what they could not find at hand. To fulfill their vision of elegance, they looked back through time and across the seas that they, or their antecedents, had crossed, borrowing from classical antiquity to create their new world paradise.

"It is in the very heart of the city . . . that one encounters the most charming surprise of this sort," wrote Lafcadio Hearn in the late nineteenth century. "Entering a paved archway . . . you suddenly find . . . a musical fountain, whose marble basin is made verdant with water plants and flowers. Above, Hebe stands ever youthful in bronze, pouring nectar into her shapely cup; swan-birds curve stony necks at her feet, and about the lower basin four sinewy Tritons, whose nervous thighs end gracefully in dolphin-tails, blow mightily through marble horns. It is delightful to meet these fragmentary dreams of antique art,—these fancies of that older world which is yet ever young with the youth of immortality,—thus hidden like treasures in the city's bosom."[1]

PAGE 134: A nineteenth-century English holder for fireplace matches contains Japanese chopsticks in orange lacquer given to Rosemary James by a cherished friend.

OPPOSITE: French Empire lamps, a Louis XV crystal chandelier, and Régence *lis-de-repos* grace the music room at the Williamson/LeBlanc house in the Garden District.

[1]Lafcadio Hearn, quoted in S. Frederick Starr, ed., *Inventing New Orleans: Writings of Lafcadio Hearn* (Jackson, Miss.: University Press of Mississippi, 2001), p. 41.

Memento Vivendi

The Strachan Family House

A GARDEN DISTRICT GREEK REVIVAL MANSION

THE RUINED TEMPLES THAT INSPIRED THE GREEK REVIVAL STYLE SO POPULAR IN THE American South stood as monuments to Gods no longer worshiped and mysteries no longer practiced behind their columned façades. It is tempting to interpret the pristine Greek Revival façade of the Payne-Forsyth-Strachan house as a monument to the faded dreams of the Old South, an interpretation fostered by the presence of a stone memorial identifying it as the place where the President of the Confederacy drew his last breath. But such a reading belies the truth of this house that has accommodated and continues to witness the vibrant lives and cherished social rituals of generations of New Orleanians.

Owned by only two families since its construction in 1849, the Strachan's house is an extremely well-preserved structure that speaks eloquently of New Orleans' past and present. Built by a cotton factor from Kentucky named Jacob Payne, the house "exudes old wealth, or so many people have thought," writes historian Fred Starr. "To be sure, when Payne died, the local press hailed him as 'one of the grandest lord masters of the old regime.' Yet this lord master had made his entire fortune in less than a decade."[1] The factor, who bought cotton from plantations up the Mississippi River and sold it to brokers in New Orleans, was also a loan agent who ultimately repossessed a number of plantations. Proceeds from these ventures funded the construction of a house that epitomized the tastes of the mid-nineteenth-century inhabitants of the Garden District.

The airy center hall house with large entertaining rooms on the ground floor and bedrooms above conforms to a five-bay London house plan favored among the Anglo-American residents of the suburban area upriver from the increasingly commercial neighborhood called the American Sector. The façade, with its tall entablature and double gallery of Ionic columns surmounted by Corinthian columns, is a clear expression of the Greek Revival style that

OPPOSITE: Built in the Greek Revival style that enjoyed prolonged popularity in New Orleans' Garden District, the Strachan house was one of the first to receive column capitals made of cast iron, manufactured in New York in 1848. This house is considered one of the finest examples of Greek Revival architecture in the neighborhood.

[1] S. Frederick Starr, *Southern Comfort: The Garden District of New Orleans* (New York: Princeton Architectural Press, 1998), p. 39.

enjoyed popularity in New Orleans well after it faded in the Northeast. Cast iron, a material that revolutionized the appearance of New Orleans' streets in the mid-nineteenth century, forms the Ionic capitals of the porch that are embossed with the date and place of their manufacture: 1848, New York.

The interior of the house also bears a Northeastern imprint, with decorative moldings copied from popular design manuals including Minard Lefever's *The Modern Builders Guide*, published in Newark in 1833. Ionic pilasters decorate the walls of entertaining rooms crowned with ornate plaster medallions and cornices adorned with wreaths. But despite these influences, the house has a distinctly Southern appearance, thanks in part to the deep two-story porch that shades its façade.

Jefferson Davis, president of the Confederacy, was a frequent visitor to the Payne house, where his daughter Winnie made her debut in 1883 and attended Mardi Gras balls, reigning as Queen of both Momus and Comus. These glittering events took place well after the Civil War, in which Payne lost nearly all his property.[2] They reveal how firmly the South in general and New Orleans in particular clung to its traditions despite drastic changes to its social and economic landscape.

Davis died in the house of his faithful friend in 1889, succumbing to pneumonia. He spent his last days "in a lovely and cheery apartment, into which the southern sun streams nearly all day," according to contemporary newspaper accounts. Although the house has changed hands once and several generations have lived there since this event, the room still bears the unintended aura of a shrine. Payne died eleven years after his friend, leaving the house to his children.

---

[2]Starr, p. 198 (paraphrasing *States*, March 12, 1900, p. 3).

Gilded mirrors were made in France to fit above the marble mantels when the house was constructed for cotton factor Jacob Payne and his family in 1849. The gilded and stenciled secretary was brought by the Forsyth family, who purchased the house in 1935. Rose Strachan selected the *boules de neige* chandelier in the 1940s.

His daughter continued to live there for another decade, then divided it into apartments. In 1935, she sold her home to the Forsyth family, who relocated from Virginia to New Orleans.

Just as the Payne family cherished their home for generations, so has the Forsyth family and its descendants. William and Hedwig Forsyth renovated the house when they purchased it in 1935, adding modern amenities but leaving the design of the house largely unchanged. Their daughter Rose Forsyth Strachan inherited the house where she lived with her husband Frank Strachan, the founder of the New Orleans office of a Savannah, Georgia, stevedoring company. From 1935 to the present, three generations of the same family have lived there and five generations have attended debutante, engagement, christening, or Mardi Gras parties that perpetuate the social rituals for which its rooms and gardens were designed.

Described as "a pivotal couple in the social and cultural activities of New Orleans,"[3] the Strachans participated in the rituals surrounding Mardi Gras each year. Frank reigned as King of Carnival in 1976 and Rose was crowned Queen of Mystic in the 1950s. Her paste crown, necklaces, and bracelets reside in a curio cabinet in the double parlor.

The room is also decorated with keepsakes and photographs from other memorable Carnivals when daughter Elizabeth was Queen of Comus, daughter Patricia was a maid in Rex and Queen of Twelfth Night, daughter Anne was Queen of Momus, and son Duncan appeared in a dress uniform modeled after Prince Wilhelm's of Germany.

An avid gardener who was "known in the area, indeed in the country, for her exquisite roses,"[4] Rose Strachan designed the formal gardens that surround the house with the help of landscape architect Umberto Innocenti. Closest to the house lies a formal garden arranged with boxwood parterres that overflow with her namesake flower each summer. Rose also commissioned a garden teahouse, constructed in 1960, that translates Classical elements into modern American design. Patricia and Anne remember sharing before-dinner drinks with guests in the teahouse that was for them an "after five" place, while their mother enjoyed it

ABOVE: Elaborate paste Mardi Gras regalia belonging to Rose Strachan.

OPPOSITE: Dark green pilasters break up the volumes of the library's lighter green walls while white moldings with a wreath pattern provide a crisp cornice treatment.

[3]Monica Meenan, "At Home," *Town and Country*, Vol. 134, No. 4998, Feb. 1980, pp. 123–25.
[4]Ibid.

ABOVE: Rose Strachan had the pair of twin beds in the guest room constructed from pieces of an English four-poster bed from which she had four additional matching posts copied. A photograph of Jefferson Davis, who died in the room, stands on the bedside table.

RIGHT: A blue, cream, and gold palette creates an elegant backdrop for the dining room's eighteenth-century Chippendale furniture and Irish Waterford chandelier. Family linens, crystal, and china set the table.

throughout the day as a place to read and escape from the busy house. "She was always happiest in the teahouse," Patricia recalls.

Rose Strachan also redecorated the interior of the house, painting the walls tones of blue, green, and terra-cotta that complement the crisp white moldings and provide a rich backdrop for a collection of European and American antiques. Family pieces brought by the Forsyths from Virginia and New York include a table and secretary in the parlor. Pieces collected by Rose include the eighteenth-century Chippendale chairs in the dining room and the French *boules de neige* chandelier in the parlor, named for the distinctive crystals in the shape of melting snowdrops. Portraits of both Rose and Frank hang in the library where glass-front cases hold books cherished by William Forsyth, who was a Classics scholar.

While mementos of every generation that has dwelled in the house remain—including the ornate mirrors made in France to fit above the mantels in the parlor and dining room when the house was built—the strongest presence is that of Rose. Her image hangs in the library, her needlework graces the parlor, and her carefully chosen furnishings and artwork fill the rooms. Roses bloom in the garden and fill the summer air with their scent. "She loved every room in this house," says Patricia.

Gracious Grandeur

The Home of Hal Williamson and Dale LeBlanc

A GARDEN DISTRICT ITALIANATE VILLA

"[M]Y HOUSE IS EXCELLENT FOR ENTERTAINING. NOTHING COULD BE BETTER," WROTE MRS. Nathaniel Banks in a letter dated May 13, 1864. Describing a large reception there, she continues, "Rooms crowded with elegantly dressed people . . . Fine performers on the piano and many excellent singers . . . Our parlors are grand."[1] The letter, sent at the height of the Civil War to the lady's husband, General Banks of the Federal Army, describes the confiscated house of Colonel Robert Short, a New Orleans cotton factor who fled to Kentucky on the eve of New Orleans' occupation.

The Italianate villa on a large corner lot in the Garden District was a hotly contested property during the decade following its design by renowned New Orleans architect, Irish-born Henry Howard. Colonel Short, who was born in Kentucky but followed the antebellum cotton boom to New Orleans, was familiar with Nottoway Plantation, a high-style plantation on the Mississippi River designed by Howard. Impressed by its beauty, Short contracted the architect in 1859 to build a fine villa in a similar style in New Orleans' Garden District.

The double parlors of the house Howard designed for Short copy the ballroom at Nottoway, while other aspects of the villa remain unique. The gregarious exterior with two projecting bays, for example, is an individualistic response to the corner lot. The interior arrangements of rooms is equally idiosyncratic, with a wide side hall paralleled by double parlors on one side and culminating in a cluster of rooms including a music room, a spacious stair hall, and a long rectangular dining room with a curved bay called a lantern window.

Colonel Short and his wife had barely moved into the house before they were forced to flee. The house was quickly confiscated by Federal powers after the fall of New Orleans and transformed into the executive mansion of the new Federal governor of Louisiana, Michael Hahn. As commandant of the Department of the Gulf, General Banks took possession of the house after Governor Hahn relocated. A self-made man from Massachusetts and a successful Washington politician, Banks and his wife entertained lavishly. "Anybody of importance who

OPPOSITE: The villa Henry Howard designed for Col. Robert Short combines the imposing verticality and geometric bays of Italianate design with the decorative silhouettes of cast-iron galleries and the famous cornstalk fence.

---

[1]Mrs. Banks to General Banks, May 13, 1864. N. P. Banks file, U.S. National Archives, Washington, D.C., as quoted in S. Frederick Starr, *Southern Comfort: The Garden District of New Orleans* (New York: Princeton Architectural Press, 1998), p. 193.

Corinthian columns
and pilasters dividing the
double parlors are devices
architect Henry Howard
also employed at Nottoway
Plantation, which Col.
Short admired. The rooms
are decorated with
Louisiana and French
antiques, including a pair
of large gilded pier
mirrors, one of which
reflects a nineteenth-
century portrait of
a Creole lady by
François Bernard.

ABOVE: A Louis XVI table fills the long dining room, while a smaller table more appropriate for intimate parties is tucked into the lantern window that overlooks the garden.

came to town in those days—including President Grant and General Sherman—was entertained here," says the house's current owner, Hal Williamson. "Sarah Bernhardt sang in the garden, Julia Child and Lee Bailey have cooked in the kitchen, and Pablo Casals played in the music room," he continues, listing nineteenth- and twentieth-century visiting celebrities.

Unlike many neighbors who permanently lost their properties and fortunes during the Civil War, Colonel Short successfully petitioned for the return of his home in 1866 and reestablished himself in business, this time as a distiller of spirits. Mr. Williamson, who is an antiques dealer and interior designer, and his domestic partner, physician Dale LeBlanc, studied photographs of the house during the post–Civil War residence of the Shorts, who decorated it in high Victorian style. Later photographs reveal the house's mid-twentieth-century appearance, when residents hired architect Samuel Wilson to add a service wing to the house.

When Mr. Williamson and Dr. LeBlanc toured the house in 1994, they barely got through the front door before deciding to buy it. Even though the Garden District was experiencing an exodus as a result of the late twentieth-century New Orleans crime wave, the two recognized the property's inherent value and irresistible charm. During the years they devoted to restoring it, the neighborhood has again become "one of the most desirable places to live in the city," says Mr. Williamson.

The restoration of the famous cornstalk fence, the house's best-known feature and the most famous cast-iron fence in New Orleans, took two-and-a-half years. The fence was purchased by Colonial Short from Wood, Miltenberger and Company, the New Orleans office of a Philadelphia-based company that flourished during the Crescent City's decades-long infatuation with cast-iron decoration. The house also has copious iron elements attached to its façade, including several galleries with fluted colonnettes and balconies with lacey silhouettes.

The interior restoration, masterminded and supervised by Mr. Williamson, has unfolded in several phases. Fortunately, the house's Union occupiers left original white marble mantels and Irish crystal and gilded French chandeliers in place. Most of the decorative plaster and woodwork—including cornice moldings in a variety of patterns and fluted interior columns—was also intact.

When it came to decorating, the designer chose a natural palette drawn from his Louisiana surroundings, including a rich bayou green and warm brown the shade of dried tobacco. Tones of yellow, gray, and ivory balance these colors, creating cool contrast to the hot subtropical sunlight that bathes the surrounding gardens. The Brunschwig & Fils wallpaper Mr. Williamson found for the stair hall after a two-

BELOW: The front parlor features delicately embellished decorative objects such as a pair of Fabergé eggs including a pale green one made in 1913 to commemorate three hundred years of the Romanov Dynasty.

year search brings these tones together, while also uniting the cornstalk design of the fence with the French Empire swan motif of the dining room's original chandelier and sconces.

A subtle grisaille color scheme covers the walls of the dining room, against which the walnut of a nine-leaf Louis XVI table and set of twenty-four caned Régence chairs glows warmly. Incandescent notes are provided by burnt-orange-patterned Fortuny curtains and a painting of the Proteus parade by New Orleans artist Tim Trapolin. "I just love that painting," says Mr. Williamson. "You get the sense of the beautiful glow of the nighttime parade, the sparkle of the foil on the floats, a kind of golden shimmer."

While paintings by other local contemporary artists including George Schmidt also hang in the house, the collection features primarily antiquarian paintings from Louisiana artists including Alexander Drysdale, Ellsworth Woodward, and Clarence Millet. Paired portraits, c. 1857, by Anatole Lucas depicting French Louisiana settlers grace the house, the wife greeting guests in the entrance hall and her husband presiding over the music room. An 1859 American piano decorated with satinwood inlay, gilding, and painted vignettes and an early-nineteenth-century Lion and Healy harp stand in the music room where a *lis-de-repos* covered in softly faded velvet offers an ideal place to listen.

A sitting area that flows into the stair hall celebrates the literary arts, with a Louis XVI biblioteque towering against one wall and a marble-topped table providing a reading surface well illumined by tall windows. A Louis Philippe carpet with a Greek key border and a pattern of faceted jewels adds opulent tones of purple and gold to the space. A lighter palette and more delicate furnishings characterize the double parlors, which are exquisitely decorated with Louis XVI and XV sofas, chairs, and tables. Irish crystal chandeliers sparkle in the two rooms, their diamond highlights bright against the pale gold walls and more deeply burnished tones of silk upholstery.

"Nearly everything we bought for the house was found in New Orleans," says Mr. Williamson, including a pair of French pier mirrors that hang above the Italian marble mantels and a rare *campeche* chair on rockers. The residents constantly share their house through entertainments that continue its tradition of grand hospitality. "As much as we like small gatherings of friends and family, we find ourselves often throwing parties with hundreds of people formally dressed," says Mr. Williamson. "If you are going to live in such a place of local as well as national importance," Dr. LeBlanc explains, "you have an obligation to care for it, share it, and preserve it for the enjoyment of future generations."

Living Rock

The Home of Mrs. and Mrs. George Villere

AN UPTOWN RICHARDSONIAN ROMANESQUE MANSION

THE HOUSE AT THE CORNER OF ST. CHARLES AVENUE AND VALENCE STREET—A CASTLE OF stone standing squarely upon a man-made hill—is a fitting monument for a man described as being as romantic as Sir Galahad or Don Quixote yet "practical in everything."[1] Dubbed King Cotton for his financial leadership, William Perry Brown led not one but two successful campaigns to corner the cotton market during the first decade of the twentieth century. A self-made man who began his career as a clerk in a Mississippi country store, he died the wealthiest man in New Orleans in 1914 and was widely mourned throughout the South, a region he greatly benefited throughout his career.

Upon his first successful cornering of the market, when Brown drove the price of cotton up from five cents a pound to twelve in 1902, he commissioned the Louisiana architectural firm of Favrot & Livaudais to design a home for his growing family. The house was intended to fulfill a wedding promise Brown made to his bride, offering her the finest house in New Orleans. Despite this boasting offer, Brown and his architects insisted that the interior of the house was designed not for show, but for the comfort of his family.[2]

In keeping with both claims, the house is as functional as it is fantastical, a grandiloquent essay in architectural solidity and sensibility, which may perhaps account for its survival in the Uptown St. Charles Avenue area where many other similarly opulent residences have fallen to the wrecker's ball. Designed in the style named for Henry H. Richardson, the New Orleans–born architect who rose to architectural fame through the popularity of his Romanesque structures, the Brown–Villere house is constructed of double-layer brick walls faced with rough-cut limestone.

"This house really keeps its temperature, hot or cold," remarks current resident Fran Villere, who has lived there with her husband, George, for twenty years. "It's probably the best insulated house in the city." She demonstrates another of the house's many practical details:

OPPOSITE: The limestone façade of the Richardsonian Romanesque house built for William Perry Brown, though symmetrical, offers lively surface variation with the warm honey-colored stones laid in both coursed and random patterns and the whole topped with a red-tile roof.

[1] *The Book of Louisiana* (New Orleans, *The New Orleans Item*, 1916), pp. 112–13.

[2] "W. P. Brown's New Avenue Home, Which Is to Be Made the City's Finest Residence Building," (New Orleans, *The Daily Picayune*, Sept. 1, 1903), n.p.

ABOVE: A winged sculpture by New Orleans artist George Dunbar stands at the base of the majestic staircase.

OPPOSITE: A sculpture's marriage of feminine forms with a robustly masculine surface echoes the aesthetic balance of the surrounding architecture.

retractable louvered shutters fitted to every window, which, she explains, "provide a way to enjoy a breeze and still have privacy." Other practical amenities that must have delighted Brown's wife included hot-air heating in every room, bathrooms adjacent to every bedroom, electric lighting, and electric call signals for summoning servants.

The exterior of the house, with its low, wide arches, compact columns, and rugged stone facing, exudes the robust masculinity associated with the Richardsonian Romanesque. But the interior offers a pleasing balance of feminine details including delicate Beaux Arts–style plaster garlands on the parlor ceiling and painted-glass windows detailed with vases of translucent roses and daisies. The latter, known as marguerites in French, were a tribute to Brown's wife, née Marguerite Braughn.

In keeping with typical plans of Richardsonian Romanesque and Queen Anne style houses, the ground floor features several entertaining rooms radiating from a cavernous hallway that doubles as additional entertaining space. The floors of each room reveal different patterns of hardwood parquet. Wood paneling with fine millwork molding, including dentils, egg-and-dart motifs, and scrolled shields ornaments the walls. Ceilings of carved and molded plaster or milled wood, each distinct in design, crown the spacious rooms. The French delicacy of the parlor contrasts with the austere paneling of the dining room; the baronial grandeur of the living hall gives way to the relative intimacy of a billiard room decorated with linen-fold paneling and a simply ornamented breakfast room that is hidden from public view.

Despite these attractions, Mrs. Villere found the interior's palette of dark, unpainted wood oppressive when she first viewed the house. Although previous residents had attempted to lighten up the interior by adding gilding, pastel murals, ultrasuede wall coverings, pink shag carpeting, and a plethora of chandeliers and wall-sconces, these efforts only competed with the original details, creating visual cacophony. Overwhelmed, the prospective buyer invited her friend and interior designer Lucile Andrus to offer an opinion about the house's livability for a late twentieth-century family. After lengthy deliberation, Mrs. Andrus announced, "Yes, dear, I think we can work with it."

Mrs. Andrus's most dramatic suggestion was to paint the walls in varying shades of cream in order to brighten the interior and highlight the exceptionally detailed millwork. "We pained over every drop of paint we brushed on," recalls Mr. Villere, who opposed the idea at first. "But the place was way too dark and fairly frightening." With three young children and a growing collection of contemporary art, the couple finally decided that lighter, brighter walls were essential.

In order to further brighten the interior, the Villeres heeded the advice of their architect, Leonard Salvato, engaging a lighting consultant to illuminate the interior without obtrusive light fixtures. At the recommendation of the New York firm of Cline Bettridge Bernstein, a system of recessed lighting hidden in the walls and ceilings was installed to subtly brighten the rooms and highlight decorative details. While making these modifications, the Villeres also hired craftspeople to restore the woodwork to its original perfection.

When the couple turned their attention to landscaping, they worked with their landscape architect René Fransen and the geology department of the University of New Orleans to locate the Ohio quarry from which the house's original limestone facing was cut. They then

purchased matching stone to construct a pavilion that perfectly reflects the house's rough-hewn surface. Below the pavilion, a series of terraces with water elements gently falls away from the level of the house.

Like the Browns before them, the Villeres enjoy the many facets of their magnificent home. Family gatherings fill the rooms with feasting and grandchildren ride scooters and tricycles across the floors. Mr. Villere, the descendent of an old New Orleans family that includes an early nineteenth-century governor of Louisiana, and his wife, who traces her ancestry to seventeenth-century French Canadians, host frequent events for civic institutions and formal dinners in the dining room that comfortably seats eighteen. A portrait portraying Mr. Villere in full Carnival regalia as King of Mystic overlooks the library where the man called "King Cotton" once relaxed with his books and newspapers.

"Since the Romanesque Revival style was already a highly eclectic style, we feel that there is no real sacrilege in adding twentieth and now twenty-first century elements to the property," says Mr. Villere. Describing the romantic structure that has so successfully bridged a century filled with aesthetic, sociological, and technological change, he adds, "This was—and still is—a very livable house."

House of Dreams

The Home of Joe and Jessie Scalia

AN EARLY TWENTIETH-CENTURY HOUSE ON ALGIERS POINT

LONG BEFORE HE BUILT HIS DREAM HOUSE, CHARLES CIEUTAT BEGAN COLLECTING RARE PIECES of highly grained cypress and shaping them into the decorative woodwork that would eventually grace it. The owner of a wood mill on Algiers Point, a spit of land just across the Mississippi River from the French Quarter, Cieutat found ready clients among his working and middle class neighbors who were building houses in Eastlake, Queen Anne, and Colonial Revival styles to replace those that perished in a destructive fire in 1895.

Not satisfied with the appreciation of his neighbors alone, mostly workers for Algiers Point's booming dry docks and a railroad line that linked the Atlantic and Pacific coasts, Cieutat created show pieces to exhibit further afield. In 1884, he displayed a robustly embellished staircase including burled cypress panels, carved shells, and turned spindles in the 1884 World's Fair held in New Orleans. In 1907, he entered a collection of decorative millwork featuring burled and even rarer bird's-eye cypress that took first prize in the Louisiana State Fair.

Having won the accolades he sought, Cieutat then built a home to house his prize-winning millwork. He chose a surprisingly restrained exterior design for his home, opting for a simple two-story frame house that combined the asymmetrical, shingled gables of the Queen Anne style with a porch whose Doric columns add a Colonial Revival note to the façade. But Cieutat was reserving his greatest ornamental impulses for expression within the house, whose decoration explores aspects of Arts and Crafts design.

"This house has some of the finest millwork of any house of its period in New Orleans," says Louis Aubert, ASID, an interior designer and color expert whose family has lived on Algiers Point since the 1840s. But when Joe and Jessie Scalia first saw the house thirty years ago, they had no idea how truly fine the woodwork was. "All the wood had a crazed black surface that completely hid the grain," Dr. Scalia remembers. The house, which had been divided into three apartments during the Depression, also direly needed new plaster and paint. But something about the house captured the Scalias' imagination.

When first seeing the house, Mrs. Scalia exclaimed, "I love it; let's buy it!" Even though the house was not on the market, the couple begged to be notified if it ever was. When the

OPPOSITE: The façade of the house built for Charles Cieutat combines the lively asymmetry of the Queen Anne style with the dignity of Doric columns. Behind the façade, robust Arts and Crafts style details abound.

FOLLOWING: Cypress paneling and plaster line the walls of the dining room where Arts and Crafts style border prints from inspired the peacock blue and plum palette.

house was offered six months later, the owner remembered the Scalias and gave them advance notice. "She couldn't stay here any more, but she wanted someone who really loved the house to own it," Dr. Scalia recalls. Although the Scalias had just bought a Greek Revival house nearby, they leapt at the opportunity to own the quaintly elegant house on Delaronde Street. They decided to use it as a rental property until they could move into it themselves when their children left home.

In preparation for tenants, the Scalias repaired the plaster and painted the walls a neutral white. They replaced many of the fixtures with antiques appropriate to the period and began to restore the wood. Working nights and weekends, Dr. Scalia and the family gently bathed the age-darkened wood with rags dipped in a mixture of lacquer thinner and shellac thinner to remove the old finish without damaging the grain. Slowly they revealed the burled and bird's-eye panels. Finally late one night, working alone in the empty house, Dr. Scalia stood back, and exclaimed, "Mr. Cieutat, you really knew your stuff."

Twenty years later, the Scalias finally claimed their dream house as their own. They removed the partition walls and hired a neighboring master carpenter, Willie Bourgeois, to create replacements for missing wooden elements that are indistinguishable from Mr. Cieutat's originals. Mrs. Scalia decided how to arrange the antique furniture she and her husband had been collecting since their early married days—a collection of mid- to late-nineteenth-century pieces that complement the house's late Victorian feel.

While they agreed easily about furniture arrangements, the couple differed on how to decorate the walls. Dr. Scalia envisioned neutral tones that would not compete with the house's colorful stained-glass windows. "I'm a very quiet Italian when it comes to color," he laughs. But Mrs. Scalia recalls, "I had a fit. This house deserves color." So the

couple turned to former neighbor Louis Aubert for advice. Mr. Aubert, who has advised on color selections for hundreds of houses in New Orleans and beyond and volunteered as a color consultant for the Preservation Resource Center's Rebuilding Together project, had ample experience.

The designer first suggested an understated palette for the exterior. "Why don't you do the outside very simply, in shades of white, so no one will guess the jewel box of colors within?" he proposed. Dr. Scalia recalls that his wife's face fell at this suggestion. "Louis, I think Jessie wants her jewels all hanging out," he commented. So the exterior was painted in shades of muted cranberry, dark plum, and slate blue that provide hints of the chromatic richness within.

To Mr. Aubert's expert eye, the robust woodwork and intensely hued stained-glass windows overwhelmed the light tones then covering the interior walls. He recommended colorful walls and figured wallpaper borders in late Victorian period designs by Bradbury & Bradbury. Once he and his clients agreed upon the borders (a total of nine layers combine to create the first parlor's elaborate cornice treatment), colors were selected that bridged the tones of the wallpaper and the wood details.

Salmon walls and a sky blue ceiling create an elegant palette in the parlors. A dusky mauve provides warm contrast to the blue and green glass of the entrance hall. For the dining room, Mr. Aubert recommended two shades of peacock blue and a plum-colored ceiling. "I thought, 'Talk about clashing!'" Dr. Scalia recalls. But once he held the wallpaper to the wall, he realized that the border brought it all together.

While the style is different, the final feel of the restored house reminds Dr. Scalia of the nineteenth-century homes he admired in the New Orleans of his youth, where owners had held onto generations-worth of furniture despite the deprivations of the Depression. "I realized what a gracious lifestyle it was, these families living in their old houses with their old furniture," he muses. "I don't know . . . I think I might have lived a long time ago. I've always loved this way of life."

PRECEDING: In the master bedroom, a vibrant violet hue complements the soft colors of the stained-glass doors.

ABOVE: A mirror reflects Charles Cieutat's finely milled staircase.

OPPOSITE: Border prints create an elaborate cornice treatment in the first parlor.

Pentimento

The Home of Mr. and Mrs. William Christovich

A GARDEN DISTRICT ITALIANATE VILLA

THE GILMOUR-PARKER HOUSE RISES AMID A VERDANT LAWN AND NEATLY TRIMMED GARDEN beds, set well back from the street behind a cast-iron fence that forms a delicate yet definite boundary between public and private grounds. A conservative exploration of the Italianate style, the house presents a nearly symmetrical pink stucco façade whose only overt Italian reference is a pair of round-arched windows on the second floor. Otherwise, the five-bay, center hall residence constructed in 1853 bears close resemblance to its Greek Revival neighbors—a comparison that would have been much stronger had builder Isaac Thayer's original plans for a pillared and galleried façade been fulfilled.

In all these details, plus the fact that it was constructed for an English cotton broker, Thomas Corse Gilmour, the house on Prytania Street is a quintessential expression of the ethos and aesthetics of New Orleans' Garden District. In intentional contrast to the tightly clustered, urban setting established by the Creole residents of the Vieux Carré and downriver faubourgs, the Garden District was established as a bucolic suburb for well-to-do English and American families. Each house was a country manor and Classic revival styles reigned from the 1820s to the 1880s, as Greek Revival gradually gave way to Italianate as the most popular mode of design.

The architectural homogeneity of the Garden District and its peaceful suburban air masked the financial and political volatility that defined it and its denizens—high rollers in a New World economy that spawned and devoured fortunes with astonishing alacrity. The London-born Gilmour made enough money to build his Prytania Street villa in just three years by buying cotton from factors, who bought it from upriver plantations, and selling it to buyers in Liverpool and continental European textile centers.[1] Although bankruptcies and seizure of real estate were common among his Garden District contemporaries, Gilmour fell victim to political rather than economic pressures less than a decade after moving into his mansion.

[1]S. Frederick Starr, *Southern Comfort: The Garden District of New Orleans* (New York: Princeton Architectural Press, 1988), p. 39.

OPPOSITE: Italianate elements including round-arch paired windows (not shown) balance a Greek revival door surround on the façade of this transitional villa designed by Isaac Thayer for English cotton broker Thomas Gilmour in 1853.

ABOVE: This depiction of
Mrs. Christovich's great-
great-grandfather was
cut out of a larger family
portrait.

OPPOSITE: A serpentine
staircase was re-created at
the rear of the stair hall,
separated from the front
with a pair of fluted
columns, which mark the
end of the original hall.

Refusing to swear the oath of American allegiance imposed upon citizens of New Orleans upon its surrender to Union forces in 1862, Gilmour took his family back to England. At first, he leased his New Orleans home to his business partner John M. Parker, Sr., father of a Louisiana governor. Two decades later, Gilmour sold the Prytania Street residence to Parker's wife, who purchased it with an inheritance and remodeled it to her own late nineteenth-century tastes. "I call it Mrs. Parker's house," says current resident, architectural historian and preservationist Mary Louise Christovich, who lives there with her husband William. "I would have loved to have known her," she adds.

One receives the impression that Mrs. Parker was heartily sick of the restrained refinement of her neoclassical residence and yearned for the bolder styles of the late Victorian era. Records reveal that she ripped out the delicately curving staircase in the center hall to replace it with a chunky Eastlake one. Similarly, she swapped large panes of plate glass, popularized in the 1884 World Exposition held in what is now Audubon Park, for the nine-over-nine mullioned windows original to the house. She installed gilded cornice boards in the parlors and a new hexagonal dining room with a large bedroom above at house's rear.

"This is Mrs. Parker's chandelier," Mrs. Christovich says, indicating the eight-branch gilded gasolier that illumines the dining room. The remainder of the chandeliers on the first and second floors—including several more gilded gasoliers with etched glass globes—were purchased by Mrs. Christovich, whose late twentieth-century interpretation of the house combines elements of both the Gilmours' and Mrs. Parker's tastes. "It's impossible to interpret this house to any one period in its history," she explains. "Houses are like people; they change!"

While she retained many of Mrs. Parker's innovations, Mrs. Christovich asked restoration architect Samuel Wilson, Jr. to recreate the Gilmours' serpentine staircase as well as mid-nineteenth-century style plaster moldings in the parlors. The Christoviches also appended their own addition to the house: a large, modern kitchen and a sunroom that opens the rear of the house to views of the surrounding garden. The original 1853 service wing

Mrs. Christovich found a nineteenth-century gilded mirror in a Magazine Street antique shop that fit perfectly above the original marble mantel in the villa's grand parlor. A nineteenth-century American portrait of a lady hangs in the corner, its surface altered at the request of the owner, who asked a restoration artist to paint out a goiter disfiguring the subject's face.

173

provides another library and sitting room. For the most part, Mrs. Christovich's decorations lean toward the mid- to late nineteenth century, dominated by stately mahogany furniture in the Empire style she purchased in New Orleans, Savannah (whose Anglo-American residents had similar tastes), and Washington, D.C.

Paint analysis revealed that the plaster walls once bore an oyster-colored shade of white, popular among mid-nineteenth-century New Orleanians including the Baroness Micaëla de Pontalba, who used it in her Vieux Carré townhouses on Jackson Square. The current owner recreated the formula and employed it throughout the house. Reproduction carpets from Patterson, Flynn & Martin and Scalamandre cover the floors with intricate patterns of gold, crimson, and black threads—rich tones that are echoed in period-style Brunswig & Fils satins, silks, and horsehair fabrics. Gilded gasoliers, cornice boards, and picture frames provide gleaming details without overpowering spacious rooms that easily accommodate such imposing accoutrements.

"This house just seems to *absorb* things," Mrs. Christovich notes, indicating two recently commissioned portraits by New Orleans artist Tim Trapolin. While these depict the current residents with immediately recognizable likenesses, the walls are also hung with paintings of what Mrs. Christovich refers to as instant relatives. "We call him Uncle Roy," she says, pointing to an early nineteenth-century oil of a handsome dark-haired man that hangs in the dining room. Two exquisite renderings of young ladies by the French artist Brochart grace the entrance hall, while a slightly primitive American portrait hangs in a corner of the grand parlor.

"That beautiful woman had a goiter!" exclaims Mrs. Christovich. "No one would buy her. We lived with that goiter for ten years, and finally, I had it painted out." She hastily adds that the artist used translucent paint that could easily be removed should later owners wish to return the painting to its original appearance. Just as a skilled art historian might discover the painting's pentimento decades from now, so a trained architectural historian can read the many layers of the Gilmour-Parker house. Such study reveals not only the differences of the generations who have inhabited the house, but also the common threads that bind them: a love of antique forms combined with a desire for modern comforts—a marriage that produced the domestic values of the Garden District and has fostered its continued livability today.

Bibliomania

Faulkner House Books and the Home of Rosemary James and Joseph DeSalvo

A FRENCH QUARTER CREOLE TOWNHOUSE

WHEN CASUAL STROLLERS AND DETERMINED BIBLIOPHILES ENTER THE GROUND-FLOOR ROOMS of Faulkner House, they are engulfed by the paper-and-ink residue of literary New Orleans. Alternately colorful and time-mellowed spines of new books and rare editions fill the shelves of antique cypress that line a brick-floored room where William Faulkner wrote his first novel, *Soldiers' Pay*, in 1925. In Faulkner's day, this apartment was dark and damp—a place inspiring introversion and offering sanctuary. But today, it is a book lover's paradise. Stacks of books cover an antique French walnut partners table and velvet-clad armchairs invite readers to linger and browse. More volumes, mostly first editions, line the hallway beyond, carefully stored behind glass doors made from windows salvaged during a renovation of the nearby Presbytère.

Those invited to ascend to the upper floors of this four-story townhouse find themselves ensconced in another New Orleans—the sensual, decadent city where French elegance and subtropical torpor combined to beguile Faulkner and many other authors. Richly upholstered French furniture graces intimately scaled rooms that fill with light. A soft green glow filters in from the courtyard at the rear of the house and bright light dances in from triple-hung windows with balconies on the façade overlooking Saint Anthony's Garden.

After successfully completing *Soldiers' Pay*, and finding inspiration for several other novels, Faulkner followed the advice of his friend and mentor, Sherwood Anderson, who also mined New Orleans' rich literary vein. He returned to Mississippi to write his most famous works, leaving behind the city he labeled "a seductress."[1] In renovating the house where Faulkner briefly lived and worked, Rosemary James and Joseph DeSalvo have succeeded in conjuring both the introversion and the seduction that helped launch the Pulitzer Prize–winner's phenomenal career.

Mr. DeSalvo, a book collector and former attorney, held a lifelong dream of opening and operating a rare bookshop. Ms. James, an interior designer, marketing consultant, and former journalist, was an active partner in launching Faulkner House Books in 1990. She also

OPPOSITE: **Rare books, including coveted editions by and about Samuel Johnson and James Boswell, along with famous American authors, fill the bookshelves of Joe DeSalvo's office. The Directoire desk with delicate inlay and bronze ormolu decoration faces a small courtyard filled with tropical plants.**

[1]Turner, Newell, "Literary Translation," *Metropolitan Home* (February 1992), pp. 70–73.

OPPOSITE: Although it is in the center of the narrow townhouse, this library is illuminated from three sides—through glazed interior walls opening onto the stairway, a transom over a door opening onto the hall, and tall windows in the adjacent salon.

created the annual Words & Music literary festival and writers' conference sponsored by the nonprofit organization the couple founded. The two divided their time between a French Quarter Creole cottage and a Victorian house on Lake Pontchartrain when they spied a For Sale sign in front of the townhouse on Pirate's Alley. A literary landmark on a quiet pedestrian way leading to Jackson Square, it provided the perfect location to fulfill their aspirations. But the dilapidated structure also posed numerous challenges.

"The house had been wrecked by moisture," Ms. James exclaimed. "It had been chopped up—if you can believe it for a tall, skinny house like this—into five apartments." Most of the original millwork, including the mantels, had been destroyed or removed. Fortunately, the previous owner had taken out most of the damaged plaster and repointed the bricks. "I think he just got bored with it," surmises the interior designer, who recognized the delicate beauty hidden behind layers of thoughtless remodeling.

The house stands on the site of the Colonial Prison, declared surplus in 1830 and purchased by Melassie LaBranche, the wealthy widow of a sugar planter who built townhouses for herself and acquaintances. A gracefully arching staircase and vestiges of millwork testify to the elegance of the structure she completed in 1837. When Faulkner arrived in New Orleans, the house was occupied by architect and silversmith William Spratling, who befriended the writer and leased him a space.

Taking cues from Creole townhouses of the same period, Ms. James devised floor plans that respected the original design while providing a kitchen, several bathrooms, a dressing room, and copious storage. According to the residents' research, the original townhouse was true to the Creole pattern in that it lacked interior hallways and featured a staircase in an extension at the rear. A service building rose to one side of the townhouse, and a courtyard opened between them. Prior to Faulkner's sojourn, the structures were linked, creating hallways and additional rooms between the two.

Today, the utilitarian functions still take place in the former service wing, which contains book storage on the first floor, a kitchen above, and bathrooms on the third and fourth floors. The created space between the two structures now houses Mr. DeSalvo's office, a dining room above, and a dressing room above that. These rooms feel almost like open-air galleries. While Mr. DeSalvo's office opens directly onto the courtyard with French windows, the dining room above has a wall of windows reflected by a bank of antique mirrored cupboards on the opposite wall.

Natural light fills the stairwell, which is enclosed by glazed interior walls and doors that invite the courtyard's glow to brighten adjacent rooms. The soft illumination creates a silvery sheen like the surface of antique mercury glass in the library, a rectangular room with

Rosemary James devised
ways to magnify existing
light in this 1837 row
house. In the airy dining
room overlooking the
courtyard, a wall lined with
antique mirrored doors
conceals storage for linens
and tableware.

a wall of bookshelves and comfortable seating including a Louis XVI provincial chaise longue, two Louis XVI chairs, and a Louis XVI canapé. The adjoining salon is similarly furnished with French antiques upholstered with sumptuous fabrics: satin both solid and striped and faux-leopard velvet. Tooled and embossed leather covers a nineteenth-century English screen, books and bibelots cluster on tables, and lamps scatter about the room, providing reading light wherever it is needed.

The French furniture provides flexible seating in a suite of rooms that frequently accommodates fifty to a hundred people for readings and receptions. The couple had an enviable collection of English and American furnishings when they purchased the house, but Ms. James explains, "The scale was all wrong, way too oversized, so we had to sell everything and start over. You can stuff a lot of French chairs into a room that would be dominated by a Chippendale chair. And frankly, French chairs are more comfortable."

While Mr. DeSalvo's distinctly masculine touch pervades his office, an intense femininity infuses the third floor's bedroom, boudoir, and dressing room. French furnishings, some painted and upholstered, others wood-stained and caned, fill the rooms. A long swath of sepia-colored wool challis hangs from the ceiling, forming a *ciel-de-lit* for the Louis XVI bed. A carved wooden putto cavorts on a swing beneath it. "I love putti," Ms. James confesses, who found a late eighteenth-century Italian chandelier of painted wood decorated with putti to provide a focal point.

The staircase grows narrower and steeper as it winds to the top floor, a loftlike space where the tastes and passions of the two residents commingle comfortably. Antique French and Italian provincial furnishings are arranged beneath exposed beams and rugged wooden trusses. Bookshelves rise from floor to high ceiling, packed with volumes of southern literature. Pretty new and antique linens cover the bed tucked beneath the eaves, offering contrast to the deep apricot glaze of the walls.

The result is a room which, like the house itself, appeals to men and to women, to literati and aesthetes, to New Orleans natives steeped in the city's southern cosmopolitanism and visitors from afar who are seduced by its exotic sensuality. Ms. James once described the house as "a belle, a tiny Faulknerian siren waiting to flaunt her considerable charms again." Brought to new life by the attentive hands and combined visions and skills of its two current residents, this belle is once more in complete command of her charms.

ABOVE: The residents transformed the uninsulated fourth floor into a comfortable guest room and study.

Europhilia

Soniat House Hotel and a Private Residence

THREE FRENCH QUARTER TOWNHOUSES

THE EARLY HISTORY OF NEW ORLEANS' SETTLERS—ADVENTUROUS FRENCH CITIZENS WHO prospered under a rapid succession of rulers, first French, then Spanish, French again, and finally American—is clearly written upon the bricks and mortar, wood and stone of the Soniat House. The large townhouse stands on a lot of land once owned by Ursuline nuns—the religious order whose convent across the street is one of very few structures from the French colonial era to survive the late eighteenth-century fires that swept the Quarter. While the convent—established by Louis XV and still active today—represents early French colonial architecture in its design, the Soniat House is a hybrid of Creole, American Federal, and pure New Orleans style.

The house was built by Joseph Soniat, born in 1770 as the second son of a French chevalier who came to protect the young city from Native American uprisings in 1751. When New Orleans passed from French to Spanish rule in 1763, the chevalier begged to transfer his allegiance to the King of Spain so that he might remain in the city he had grown to love. Although his first son returned to France to claim the family chateau, Joseph remained in New Orleans where he raised a family amid opulent surroundings on the Tchoupitoulas Plantation outside the city.

In 1829, Joseph contracted the builder Francois Boisdore to construct the townhouse on Chartres Street that would provide a spacious home for his wife, Louise Duralde, and thirteen children. For his prestigious client, Boisdore created a modish yet practical home in a type that was to sweep the French Quarter in the coming decade: the Creole townhouse that married the brick row house tradition of East Coast cities with the climate-conscious courtyard configuration of Creole design.

OPPOSITE: Fitted with trellis designed by Frank Masson, the entrance hall to the private townhouse creates a transitional space evocative of a shady courtyard. An eighteenth-century garden figure peaks out from around a corner.

In common with its northeastern progenitors, Soniat House presents a symmetrical, brick façade to the street with a large central entrance surmounted on the second floor by a door decorated in the Federal style with a wide fanlight and paired columns. In the original design, arched windows opened onto the sidewalk, but this typical Creole detail was erased when the heavy wrought-iron double gallery was added in the 1860s and the window arches were filled in with brick. In keeping with Creole tradition, the ground-level entrance opens not into an interior stair hall, but to a *porte cochere*, or covered carriage way, leading to the large interior courtyard. Also in the Creole manner, an exterior staircase leads to the second floor; but there, the arrangement of rooms around a wide center hall mimics the popular nineteenth-century American arrangement.

Joseph Soniat enjoyed the use of his French Quarter townhouse for twenty-two years and his widow lived on there until 1865. As the nineteenth century drew to a close and the lower French Quarter gradually lost luster, the house fell into decline. While economic lassitude prevented the destruction or alteration of most of the Quarter's nineteenth-century buildings in the first half of the next century, an early preservation ethos stirring in the mid-1940s protected them in the second half. Soniat House benefited from both trends, finding a succession of owners who preserved its basic appearance while ultimately transforming the grand residence into an inn.

According to its present-day owners, Soniat House was the first such inn to open in the French Quarter, ushering in a tide of imitators. Sixteen years later, the townhouse across the street, constructed by Joseph Soniat's son Edmond in 1834, also became an inn. Today, both structures comprise a small hotel with luxuriously appointed rooms and lush courtyards. The proprietors also own a nearby townhouse dating from the 1860s that they use as their residence.

To transform the small, understated spaces of their townhouse into well-proportioned rooms decorated in the European style, the residents hired Frank Masson, a New Orleans architect well-schooled in the city's architectural traditions, and Nicholas Haslam, one of England's foremost interior designers. Masson and Haslam, in turn, worked with a team of expert craftspeople to create exquisitely decorated entertaining rooms on the second floor and an elegant bedroom suite above.

A master carpenter from New Orleans named Lars Jenson created the fluted colonettes in the dining room inspired by the Catherine Palace near St. Petersburg. New Orleans decorative painters Jansen van der Veer gilded the dining room's leafy capitals and Helen Anderson faux-grained the walls of a small elevator; a Czech-born artist named Nominka d'Albanella painted the *verre églomisé* panels that mirror one another at the end of the grand salon; and Paul and Janet Czainksy from London created the hand-painted, gilded wallpaper that covers the salon walls. This ethnically diverse group recalls the national diversity of craftspeople that flocked to New Orleans in the late eighteenth and nineteenth centuries to fulfill its residents' insatiable demand for extravagant décor.

OPPOSITE: Paul and Janet Czainksy of London created the Chinoiserie-inspired hand-painted, gilded wallpaper in the owners' grand salon. A pair of *verre églomisé* mirrors flank the far end of the room where they reflect the room's dusky glow.

ABOVE: Silk curtains the shade of ashes-of-roses complement the muted floral tones of the hand-painted wallpaper.

ABOVE: Antique
European and American
crystal, china, and silver
set an elegant table.

OPPOSITE: The elegant
dining room was inspired
by Russian neoclassical
architecture, in particular,
an apartment in the
Catherine Palace near
St. Petersburg.

"The eighteenth century was our watchword—not too strict or raffiné, but newer, given élan, glamour, drama," says Mr. Haslam.[1] While the trelliswork and marble statuary of the entrance hall invokes the serenity of a well-shaded English garden, the grand salon's duskily gleaming surfaces seemed bathed in perpetual candlelight. A screen of fluted columns and clusters of antique furniture—most of it purchased by the residents on buying trips for Soniat House Antiques—divide the large room into intimate seating areas. Bold African textiles and contemporary paintings balance the formality of floor-length curtains cut from ashes-of-roses silk. Similarly, bookcases filled with well-thumbed volumes offset the majesty of the dining room's columned walls and ceiling mural, transforming the room into a library as well.

"We travel frequently to Europe and we always find inspiration there," says one of the residents. Like their eighteenth- and nineteenth-century predecessors in the Vieux Carré, the owners have transplanted these European ideas to the fertile banks of the Mississippi River. At both Soniat House and in their private realm, they have evoked and evolved the mélange of continental European elegance, Creole comforts, and southern hospitality that make the French Quarter such an intriguing destination, at once exotic and familiar.

---

[1]Nicholas Haslam, "New Quarters," *British Homes and Garden*, p. 165.

Reviving Revivalism

The Home of Debbie and Bobby Patrick

A METAIRIE COLONIAL REVIVAL HOUSE

THE TOWN OF METAIRIE, LOUISIANA, IS THE OLDEST AND ONE OF THE MOST POPULAR neighborhoods in the greater New Orleans metropolitan area. Taking its name from the French word for "small farms," it stands on former Indian hunting grounds that were divided into vast plantations, then later small farms and dairies. Always rural, parts of Metairie still retain a peaceful gardenesque quality that has drawn residents from New Orleans' denser downtown neighborhoods since the 1940s. That is why antiquarian and interior decorator Patrick Dunne dubbed Metairie, "the Garden District of the late twentieth century."

Built in 1953 in a neighborhood with generous green spaces and mature oak trees, the Patricks' house is a restrained expression of the Colonial Revival style. The house is constructed of soft red New Orleans brick, punctuated by mullioned windows surmounted by segmental arches. Reminiscent of a genre of Louisiana plantations that resemble the brick ones built in the upper South, the edifice of the Patricks' house borrows the graceful solidity of late Georgian and early Federal styles without aping specific period details.

Despite the house's many advantages, including proximity to schools attended by the family's four children, it presented multiple challenges including low ceiling height and a poorly organized arrangement of rooms. But under Dunne's expert direction, it was transformed into a comfortable residence, at once elegant and understated, that reflects the venerable traditions of southern domestic arrangements. Inspired by the old house inventories that abound in Louisiana, the Patricks decided their interiors should have a mix of French and Louisiana pieces, including the extraordinary collection of eighteenth- and nineteenth-century Louisiana furniture and Southern art they had already begun to amass. The final effect evokes a country manor house where several generations of a family have lived.

In order to create this look in a house barely fifty years old, the Patricks installed antique interior surfaces and details and hired craftspeople schooled in traditional Creole building trades. A master carpenter built a new staircase for the entrance hall with a hand-carved

OPPOSITE: A portrait of Maria Luisa Landreaux by Spanish-born, eighteenth-century Louisiana painter Jose Francisco Xavier de Salazar y Mendoza hangs beneath the stair.
A portrait miniature of Karoline Patrick by contemporary artist Thomas Sully sits on the antique chest of drawers. Karoline was born in 1993, two hundred years to the day after Salazar's young sitter.

railing that resembles the wavering lines of antique handrails. One-hundred-and-fifty-year-old floorboards salvaged from the University of Mississippi cover the floors of the entrance hall, gentleman's library, and a spacious drawing room. A wide cypress mantel with Federal details, dating from the early nineteenth century, adds another historic detail to the drawing room. The matte finish of exposed beam ceilings complements floors that are maintained with a nineteenth-century technique employing sand and vinegar. "The way the light hits the unfinished floors and illuminates the room is important," says Mr. Dunne.

Attention to such detail is evident throughout the house, including the original kitchen and a large family room addition. In these rooms, the old bricks that cover the floor were laid out beneath Mrs. Patrick's watchful eye. While not even the most formal rooms of the house cross the line into touch-me-not stiffness, the kitchen exudes a relaxed country air. Something is nearly always cooking—red beans and rice or shrimp gumbo—and the large table and padded rocking chair encourage tarrying, which was exactly what the Patricks envisioned.

The former utility room, transformed into a combined potting shed/wine cellar, looks as though it was beamed down in its entirety from the south of France. With terra-cotta floors, walls painted to resemble tawny stone, and a wooden door with hand-wrought hinges that hails from a castle in France, the room is whimsically theatrical. The massive door looks as though it leads to a dark stairway descending to a dungeon, but instead, it creaks open to reveal a pantry filled with bottles of fine wine, single malt scotch, and cigars.

The second-floor rooms reveal an equal commitment to invoking the unpretentious comfort and rustic elegance of a centuries-old house. Antique heart pine covers

The Louis XVI walnut dining table is set for dessert with French Vieux Paris porcelain. A Louisiana landscape by Joseph Rusling Meeker hangs above a c. 1789 walnut *buffet de chasse*. The portrait above the mahogany console is by Francois Bernard.

OPPOSITE: A gentleman's library opens off the entrance hall, its nineteenth-century American library cases filled with a collection of beautifully glazed, early-twentieth-century pottery from the kilns of Sophie Newcomb College.

RIGHT: Sunlight streams into the *cave*, a combination wine cellar and potting shed that Patrick Dunne created by refitting a former utility area with antique French tile, faux-stone wall treatments, and an eighteenth-century French wine cellar door.

the floors and ceiling. Mahogany four-poster beds, Louisiana armoires, and upholstered chairs fill the rooms. Even the youngest daughter's bedroom is furnished with antiques, including an early eighteenth-century Louisiana armoire and a large bed into which ten-year-old Karoline needs steps to climb. "It's very much a child's room of the past and the present," says Mrs. Patrick, who used her daughter's favorite colors, violet and green, for accents.

When she was Karoline's age, Mrs. Patrick loved to summer in the Mississippi countryside with her grandmothers, who still practiced many ways of an older era. "Going backwards and forwards, remembering your antecedents and caring for the next generation— that is such an important part of this family's life and has become very much part of the spirit of the place," says Mrs. Patrick. Mr. Dunne echoes her sentiments. "So many houses are decorated in a time capsule, which makes them feel stagnant," he notes. "This house feels very much alive."

Une Maison Famille

The Home of Patrick Dunne and Zoubir Tabout

A FAUBOURG MARIGNY TOWNHOUSE

OPPOSITE: In the dining room, gray, burnt orange, and pink offer a surprisingly sympathetic color scheme inspired by the Directoire screen hanging in the corner. The walls are painted what Mr. Dunne calls, "an old-fashioned idea of pink that is very flattering in candle-light to our lady guests."

THERE IS A FRENCH EXPRESSION, "UNE MAISON FAMILLE"—A FAMILY HOUSE—THAT DESCRIBES not just a structure and its residents, but also an entire way of life. "This is a house less intent on being perfect than on expressing the histories of several lifetimes," explains Patrick Dunne, an internationally known antiquarian and decorator who shares a mid-nineteenth-century dwelling designed by the renowned architect Henry Howard with his partner, Zoubir Tabout. Mr. Tabout, a French antiquarian who was born in Paris but traces his roots to Byzantine North Africa, elaborates. "*Une maison famille* is a place where generations have lived and left their imprint, where they are comfortably surrounded by things they feel a personal connection to."

This *maison famille* has been conjured in a year of intensive restoration and several more of decoration and living, rather than the usual cycle of generations, but the results so perfectly express the spirit of the phrase, they render the actual chronology irrelevant. When a magazine editor toured the house not long after Mssrs. Dunne and Tabout moved in, he asked how long they had lived there. "Guess," Mr. Dunne parried. "Ten years? Fifteen?" the visitor queried. "Cinq mois!" Mr. Tabout replied.

That Mr. Dunne is the proprietor of the Lucullus antiques stores in the French Quarter and Uptown offers one reason for the pair's success in creating such an illusion. Another factor is that both grew up in cultures with strong oral traditions. "When we decorate a house, we tell ourselves *une histoire*," explains Mr. Tabout. Thus the collections of objects, colors, and spaces they assemble become not just aesthetically pleasing arrangements, but also evocative settings where lives seemed to have been unfolding for an indeterminate period of time. Both residents also share a deep sense of continuity with old-fashioned modes of living.

"I grew up in a world that was very much linked with the past," admits Mr. Dunne, whose introduction to opera came from listening to records on a wind-up Victrola. Mr. Tabout, who grew up in a household where some customs had not changed for centuries, remembers watching his mother card and weave woolen blankets as keepsakes for her eight children. He spends hours listening to vintage recordings of early jazz, mambo, and samba played on a

BELOW: The residents
furnished the kitchen
with antiques instead of
installing built-in cabinets.
Self-designated kitchen
Luddites, they also eschew
automated appliances.

1950s portable record player. "I don't know why, but this music brings back the memories," he muses, tapping into a collective unconscious of early twentieth-century American and European leisure activity.

The scale and style of the house, an intimate side-hall townhouse that combines elements of Greek Revival elegance and Creole simplicity, provide an ideal setting for the current residents' approach to living. "This is not an attempt to create a period interior, or even a New Orleans interior," Mr. Dunne explains, "but to decorate with things that have some personal meaning to us." In a corner of the front drawing room, for example, an eighteenth-century colonial Mexican crucifix and small confessional screen from Mr. Dunne's family home in Corpus Christi, Texas, rest beneath a portrait depicting an eighteenth-century ancestor. An armchair with faded upholstery stands nearby. "We have so many photographs—and happy memories—of our family sitting in this chair," Mr. Dunne chuckles. He claims to have known the history of every tea stain on the nearby sofa until they finally reupholstered it.

The front drawing room, decorated with eighteenth-century French furniture and

paintings collected by Mr. Dunne's grandfather, flows into a second drawing room that previously served as a bedroom for Mr. Dunne's late mother. "We had a very old New Orleans arrangement, because there was always a first-floor bedroom for convalescents," Mr. Dunne comments. "When we had parties, we would leave the pocket doors ajar and she would hold court, talking and laughing." Although his mother's bed has now been moved upstairs, her beloved portraits of ladies including the Queen of Spain, the Sultana of Turkey, and Mary Magdalen remain in the room their Spanish-speaking housekeeper calls the *Sala de la Señora*.

Each room has an individual palette that unites several shades of a color. The kitchen, inspired by the old-fashioned kitchens beloved by both residents, exudes the earthy warmth of southern provinces. Originally intended as the house's dining room, the kitchen is paved with nineteenth-century French tile of glazed red clay. A large fireplace covered with rough yellow stucco dominates one end of the room. A marble pastry table stands in the center, illuminated by a French chandelier, originally kerosene burning. "For southern

people, especially in France and North Africa, the kitchen is really the heart of the house," says Mr. Tabout. "It's where everybody lives, where they stay and talk."

The French tile continues into the dining room at the rear of the house. The residents call this the summer room because of the many windows and French doors that open onto the garden. Eighteenth-century paintings depict appropriate scenes of picnicking, hunting, and other outdoor pursuits, and a screen covered with Directoire wallpaper hanging above a

ABOVE: Patrick Dunne and Zoubir Tabout replaced ill-scaled wooden mantels that had been painted pink with dark marble mantels they found in a salvage shop.

lis-de-repos gives the room its color scheme. "It's a road map to the color palette of the nineteenth century—that wonderful olive background with those brilliant oranges and pinks," Mr. Dunne exclaims. "No one today would ever think to mix those colors."

At the room's far end, a back staircase leads to a guest bedroom on the second floor wing that is decorated in dusky shades of lavender, a color Mr. Dunne recalls from childhood houses. Located in what was originally a dependency, the room exhibits spare architectural detail, including a simple mantel painted slate gray in the Creole tradition. The floor is covered with an old carpet that has been worn to the nub by generations of traffic. The bed, its foot and headboard carved with geometric floral patterns, is part of an entire suite of furniture belonging to the family. "My nephew lived with us for a year, and I believe he was the sixth generation to sleep in that bed," Mr. Dunne notes. "I think that thought weighed a bit heavily with him." Mr. Tabout's nieces also claim to have detected the otherworldly weight of the ancestors while occupying the guest rooms.

More family memorabilia, including a selection of papal medals and a much-used collection of books, fills the library, where the color scheme is green. An old Victrola stands in the room where the residents enjoy reading and listening to music in the evenings. A black-and-white photograph of Mr. Dunne's father, who used to order books from New Orleans for his home in Texas, sits on a shelf. "My father loved antiques and beautiful things," says Mr. Dunne, enumerating the cherished objects and habits he inherited from his father. Among these is a clock that once graced the Dunne family dining room. "If my father was having a good time at a dinner party, he would always stop the clock," recalls this son who inherited so many of his father's traits, not the least being a skill for stopping time and lingering in the beauty of the moment.

ABOVE: A photograph of Mr. Dunne's father, portrait miniatures of European royalty, and busts of literary and musical figures grace the library.

OPPOSITE: The Creole mantels were often painted matte gray to simulate slate, a shade that complements the lavender tones of the guest room.

Index —◦—

ACKNOWLEDGMENTS

This book could not have been completed without the generosity and assistance of many people, institutions, and businesses. Many thanks to:

Steve Case and Ellen Cohen of Rizzoli
International Publications

Shirley and C. J. Fayard

Patricia Gay

Deborah Geltman

International House

Michael Llewellyn

Moldaner's Camera

Eric Mueller and Element group

The New Orleans Metropolitan Convention and
Visitors Bureau, Inc.

Preservation Resource Center of New Orleans

Tim Trapolin

The Williams Research Center of the Historic
New Orleans Collection

Windsor Court Hotel

OPPOSITE: At Kerry Moody's Creole cottage, French doors connect the bedroom to the dining room and link both to the *gallery cabinet* beyond that now serves as kitchen and bath.

PAGES 206–207: Located in a French Quarter Creole townhouse and slave quarters dating from 1770, Lucullus antiques also includes a large courtyard where antique French garden furniture and nineteenth-century stone fountains are displayed.

PAGE 208: Shotgun houses line the side streets of the Uptown neighborhoods, their narrow façades displaying a range of ornamentation from restrained neoclassicism to decorative late Victorian styles.